LUMINOUS DARKNESS

KALOS

The word *kalos* (καλός) means beautiful. It is the call of the good; that which arouses interest, desire: "I am here." Beauty brings the appetite to rest at the same time as it wakens the mind from its daily slumber, calling us to look afresh at that which is before our very eyes. It makes virgins of us all, and of everything—there, before us, lies something that we never noticed before. Beauty consists in *integritas sive perfectio* (integrity and perfection) and *claritas* (brightness/clarity). It is the reason why we rise and why we sleep—that great night of dependence, one that reveals the borrowed existence of all things, if, that is, there is to be a thing at all, or if there is to be a person at all. Here lies the ground of all science, of philosophy, and of all theology, indeed, of our each and every day.

This series will seek to provide intelligent-yet-accessible volumes that have the innocence of beauty and of true adventure, and in so doing remind us all again of that which we took for granted, most of all thought itself.

SERIES EDITORS:
Conor Cunningham, and Joseph Terry

Luminous Darkness

The Passion of the Last Words

...

Carol Scott and Caitlin Smith Gilson

With Original Art by Carol Scott
Foreword by Conor Cunningham

CASCADE *Books* · Eugene, Oregon

LUMINOUS DARKNESS
The Passion of the Last Words

Kalos series

Copyright © 2025 Carol Scott and Caitlin Smith Gilson. All rights reserved. Except for brief quotations in critical publications or reviews, no part of this book may be reproduced in any manner without prior written permission from the publisher. Write: Permissions, Wipf and Stock Publishers, 199 W. 8th Ave., Suite 3, Eugene, OR 97401.

Cascade Books
An Imprint of Wipf and Stock Publishers
199 W. 8th Ave., Suite 3
Eugene, OR 97401

www.wipfandstock.com

PAPERBACK ISBN: 979-8-3852-1832-5
HARDCOVER ISBN: 979-8-3852-1833-2
EBOOK ISBN: 979-8-3852-1834-9

Cataloguing-in-Publication data:

Names: Scott, Carol [author] [illustrator]. | Smith Gilson, Caitlin [author]. | Cunningham, Conor, 1972– [foreword writer].

Title: Luminous darkness : the passion of the last words / Carol Scott and Caitlin Smith Gilson ; with a foreword by Conor Cunningham.

Description: Eugene, OR: Cascade Books, 2025 | Series: Kalos

Identifiers: ISBN 979-8-3852-1832-5 (paperback) | ISBN 979-8-3852-1833-2 (hardcover) | ISBN 979-8-3852-1834-9 (ebook)

Subjects: LCSH: Religious poetry, American. | Christian poetry, American. | Poetry. | Jesus Christ—Crucifixion. | Art, Modern—21st century.

Classification: PN6110.R4 S36 2025 (paperback) | PN6110.R4 (ebook)

VERSION NUMBER 03/14/25

Gallopers, Cover Art, by Carol Scott, 60" x 40" color pencil, acrylic on wood

To our friendship, families, and loves . . .

Beloved
My heart is full
Of holy thoughts
and sacred sex
for you

Exalted
My mind overflows
With venerated words and constant praise for you

Prized
My body trembles
With rapturous pleasures of you

Perfection
My soul breathes
Your spirit and I am yours

—"Beloved," by Carol Scott

Happy Hour, by Carol Scott

Contents

Tarsus, by Carol Scott xiv

Author's Note: Christ's Own Poetry: The Seven Last Words xv

You Intoxicate My Soul, by Carol Scott xxviii

Foreword by Conor Cunningham xxix

Artist and Model, by Carol Scott xxx

Acknowledgments xxxi

Hear No Evil, by Carol Scott xxxii

I. FATHER FORGIVE THEM, THEY KNOW NOT WHAT THEY DO 1

Obituary Crawfish, by Carol Scott 2

There Are Stories Older than Sin 3
My Secret 6
The Mind of the Beloved 9
Felix Culpa 11
Corpus Christi 13
Amare 15
Pouring Out 17
Need 19
Broken Down 21
If Only 23
God of Fools 26
The Metaphysics of Love 28

Forgive: The Shared Poems of Artist Carol Scott and Caitlin Smith Gilson 34

Material Desire, by Carol Scott 34

Reverie in Four Parts 35
Tossed Alive 38
All Your Light on Me 40
To Whom Do I Say Goodnight? 43
Forgive Me Love 45

II. TODAY YOU WILL BE WITH ME IN PARADISE 47

North Star, by Carol Scott 48

I Know 49
Second Sight 51
Rose Candoglia 52
I Am So in Love with You 54
The Traveler 56
Paradise 58
We Know Who We Are 60
The Moon 61
The Un-Perishing 64
The Envy of Recollection 66
You Are . . . 68
At Your Word 70

Paradise: The Shared Poems of Artist Carol Scott and Caitlin Smith Gilson 71

Stardust, by Carol Scott 71

Phantom Touch 72
Let's Break Bread 74
In All My Passion 76
Like All Good Stories 77
Goodnight Love Maker 79
Wonder What It Is Like to Be You? 81

III. WOMAN, BEHOLD YOUR SON! BEHOLD YOUR MOTHER! 85

Beautiful, by Carol Scott 86

Of Love and God 87
My Love for You Is Constant 90
You Are Creator 91
Laughter Is Good 92

Legacy of Your Rosary 94
The One Who Shares My Heart Can Make Anything 96
More than Modern 98
The Perfect Fit 100
The Friendship in Christ 102
The Foundress 104
My Child, My Little One: *Ad Jesum per Mariam* 106
The Axe and Tear 108

Behold: The Shared Poems of Artist Carol Scott and Caitlin Smith Gilson 111

City Park with the Grandsons, by Carol Scott 111

The Night of Blessings 112
You Are All Beauty to Me 115
The Vision Flowing Gold 117
Everywhere Else 119
Fate 121
The Bond of Unknowing 123
The Morning Feel of Child You 125

IV. MY GOD, MY GOD, WHY HAVE YOU FORSAKEN ME? 127

Chalices Burning, by Carol Scott 128

Last Evening Shelled the Sun 129
For the Time Being 131
My Father 133
The Weather Has Finally Shifted 136
The Winter's Chill 137
Today I Was Late 139
I Could Have Perished in My Sorrow 143
Apocalypse 145
Time 147
Forsaken 148
I am the Sorrow of Homecoming 150
Ruiner of Prayer 152

Forsaken: The Shared Poems of Artist Carol Scott and Caitlin Smith Gilson 154

The Vespers, by Carol Scott 154

I Am a Mortal Being 155
What Is It? 157
Tears Have Drowned My Soul 159
Alpha and Omega 161
Be Aware 162
Unforsaken 164

V. I THIRST 167

    Crystal and Tabasco, by Carol Scott 168

All I Need 169
Madagascar 170
Mystical Body of Christ 171
In the Days 173
Diving from the Ledge 175
Confession at Sea 176
Deferred Gratitude: A Cycle 178
The Things . . . 181
What Can I Write? 184
Split Apart 186
It Is Raining 188
Tonight Will Be the Thought of Your Hips 190
The Drum 192

    Thirst: The Shared Poems of Artist Carol Scott and Caitlin Smith Gilson 193
    The Goblets, by Carol Scott 193

Bodies Go Fire 194
The Severing in Three 195
New Life 198
The Songs of Solomon 200
One Liners 204
The Story of a Soul 206

VI. IT IS FINISHED 209

    Pinned and Pricked, by Carol Scott 210

The Velveted Cape 211
Evensong 213
What Else Can I Say 215

The Jewelry Box 217
The Image 220
The Wordless Said 222
Stratosphere 225
The God of Inscape 226
My Dream 229
The Lottery 231
Too Tired to Dream of Cities 233
The Last Faith 234

> **Finished: The Shared Poems of Artist Carol Scott and Caitlin Smith Gilson 236**
>
> *Lifesavers*, by Carol Scott 236

The Eros of the Risen Lord 237
If You Could See Me 241
Cannot Stop 245
We Are Swimming between Universes 246
Today Is the Day of All 249

VII. FATHER, INTO YOUR HANDS I COMMEND MY SPIRIT 253

> *Chandelier in Pink*, by Carol Scott 254

The Winter's Allegory 255
In the Final Month 258
When You Sway the Heavens 260
On the Train 263
Loving You Makes the Word 266
The Passing Thought 268
On the Way 271
The Body of Christ: A Cycle for You 274
The Everything About You 278
Rolled in Lotus 281
On the Hillside 283
We Do Not Know What God Has in Store 285

> **Spirit: The Shared Poems of Artist Carol Scott and Caitlin Smith Gilson 287**
>
> *Grand Chandelier*, by Carol Scott 287

When the Ghost of Me Comes 288

Today When I Left 290
Lines in Water 293
IMAGINE UTOPIA: *The Sextet* 296
What Makes Me Hold On 304
Not to Be Left Behind 306
You Have All the Power 308

HOLY SATURDAY 309

Between Heaven and Earth, by Carol Scott 310

Of Ancient Oracles: From Good Friday to the Harrowing 311
I Did Not Know 319
The Night of Fresh Squeezed Lemons 321
It Was Only One Sunset Ago 323
The Spirit 325
Of Hell 326
The Dead Sea 327
There Is Only Love and Time 329
Disjecta Membra 330
You Have Taken My Child 332
The Pinched Outer Shell 334
Below the Altars 336

Holy Saturday: The Shared Poems of Artist Carol Scott and Caitlin Smith Gilson 338

The Angel of Sorrow, by Carol Scott 338

Seven Last Words 339
This Unexpressed Heart 341
When the Colors Come 343
Life Is Surface 345
What I Mean to Say 347

POSTSCRIPT: EASTER SUNDAY 351

The Invitation of the King—Rex 1890, by Carol Scott 352

In the Time and Sky of You 353
Baptismal Font 355
Easter Vigil 357
You Need a Love Song 358
Beyond the Orchids 361

**Easter Sunday: The Shared Poems of Artist
Carol Scott and Caitlin Smith Gilson** 362

Splendid, by Carol Scott 362

You Will Always Be the Delectation 363
I Have Asked You to Haunt Me 365
Time and Birth 367

LAGNIAPPE 369

Cock's Crow, by Carol Scott 370

Always Being Told My Eyes Are Beautiful 371
For My Mother 373
Galatea's Kiss 375
Every Day Since You Were Born: For Mary & Lily 376

Full of Grace, by Carol Scott 379

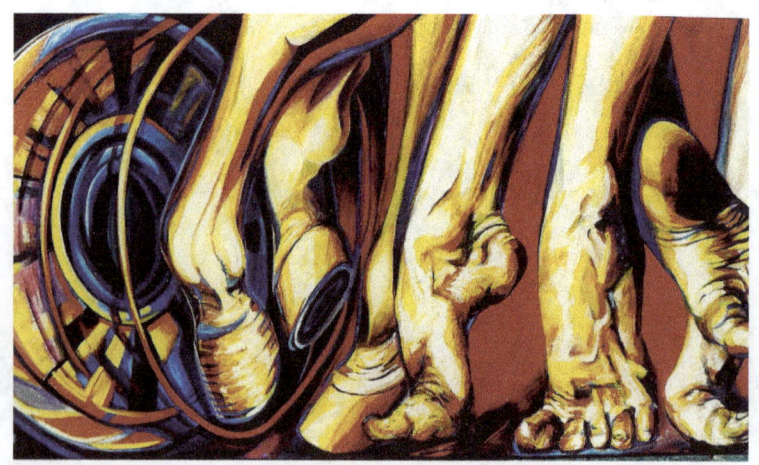
Tarsus, by Carol Scott

Author's Note

CHRIST'S OWN POETRY: THE SEVEN LAST WORDS

> Every wound of Christ strikes through His mystical Body: is a means whereby that Body is united to the Tree of Life. In so far as we are remade in His image, these wounds must strike through us too. They are the instruments of our glory, our union with Him. The friends of God are wounded in the hands that work for Him, in the feet that journey to Him, in the heart that asks only strength to love Him: as he too is wounded in His ceaseless working for us, His tireless coming to us, His ineffable desire towards us. We share the marks of His passion, and He ours. . . . "*Intra tua vulnera absconde me!*" [Within Thy wounds hide me.] No idle metaphor, no poetic image: but the grandest petition of the awakened Spirit of Life, pressing at all costs towards its home in the heart of God, the one reality.
> —Evelyn Underhill, *The Path of Eternal Wisdom*

DEATH UNVEILS THE NUMINOUS fragility of the human and divine relationship. It is the parent of extraction and removal, the great loss and gain, and it imparts its own unmistakable, generational imprint. Down the line, past time and memory, death presses itself against our anguish, becoming one with our faces. This terminus is no mere dialogic partner; it is not the other *as other* we engage. It is the enemy of the self, and its friend through the life and death of the cross. Death is the meaning and dissolution of each of us. Our dying is present and permeating all parties in every conversation—*forgive us, we do not know its extent and reaches*. We barter with its brutal and gentle intangibility that is somehow more visceral, real, elusive, terrifying, menacing, and *still* the invitation to eternal love. In dying, we can experience the true identification of reality, casting every form of realism in the light of the lesser. The things in life known for independence reveal their startling dependency. The images and memories forgotten as insignificant, reign within our dying mind. All desires become redrawn in the ebbing human drama of appearance and disappearance. And yet these innermost desires cannot be imparted, for when we die, death steals the Word. Those of us who remain give a backward glance to take in death before it takes us, but we must soon retreat and return from where we came. *What* can we say, and *how* can we say it? . . .

This collection of poetry continues the enactment of philosophy and theology *through* immediacy, particularly with reference to the apocalyptic and eschatological character of Being revealed in Christ's passion. The last words serve as mystical thoroughfare from *arche* to *telos* and always the *between*. The Seven cycles of poetry—rooted in each of Christ's seven last words—intend a *unified* philosophical and theological dwelling. Here, the poet begins from the irresistible force of finality, the very wager of existence itself, and makes herself dialogic magnet, working to draw in and draw out the core of the human and divine relationship. In this philosophical mystique, *eros* and *agape*, as totalizing risk, take on the role of guides. The cycle, in an into-the-earth filiation with the seven last words of the Passion. It is a glimpse of heaven, a companion to the liturgical givenness, and in a compact invitational beauty (*kalos*).

We are relentlessly and lovingly presented with death's ultimacy and tension in Christ. Christ overcomes death not by removing its features from the landscape of Being, but by making it the revelation of what it has always subsumed! For each of us, the same experiences are always untranslatably intimate and yet universal in the divinely human repetition of life and death which, for each, is an unrehearsed play with oft-cited lines. The truth is we are fools. We are foolish to the point of a deadening age. Too pitiful even to pity our own infirmity. Too full of pride to pray for humility. And in the absence of penitence and thanksgiving, we deny ourselves the wilderness, becoming too lost to pray. Still, we abide by the soul of the poetic, the stretched longing *poesis* that elevates and devastates. None can live and breathe immune to the countless generational ruins borne of the mystique of Being. The soul at its most humane is marked by death *as poetry*. We run towards the sacrament, towards the arms of another, to the old photographs, to the scent of the old clothing of the lover long dead, we wake up as night blooms its heavy canopy and recall the sunshine of our innocence. Even the most cynical carry some untranslated *poesis* that can resurrect the raging weeping that everyone and no one can share. Death is the one setting where nothing adds up, where the untranslated is given its full ground. Christ makes this uninhabitable *poesis his* home, the impossible but necessary home of our redemption. Christ is in agony until the end of time, until we have faces again. Our Savior speaks poetry so that we may endure death. In his dying, he gives over in languishing need the untranslated word. This is the seven last words: the death *as poetry*, the poetry that calls for immersion and alone wraps us in the cloak of heaven.

In the beginning of the passion we wait without hope, for we are not ready for hope. In revealing the supreme poetry of the seven last words, we are given the ways to bear what is beyond bearing. The cross has lifted us out of that unnaturalness of death, but this transcendence is not magic, it does not absolve the reality of the world as irredeemable without Christ's grace and mercy. This is the risk of grief when the dead child, or the lover, or the loved one is beyond our reach. The healing that comes from faith always springs from the recognition that death is a gaping wound, and all the earthly powers fall lifeless. We *must* believe, and without contradiction, that the little ones have made it home. In Christ, the holy innocents miss nothing and gain it all. We also experience the overwhelming alienation and immeasurable loss that define death carried to its fulcrum in Christ. Even our Lord asked if the cup could be passed. Heaven is home, but earth is the *way* home. The seven last words are the translated *poesis* of the paradox of death. Death is a natural experience, a profoundly unnatural state, and the estuary of supernatural life. This bewildering mystique is experienced in all daily living, and none is immune to it. Christ is the substance of poetry for he is the life of the eternally dying, the forever longing, and the consummating joy. These seeming contradictions are not managed by a rationalism but are the living experience of each person seeking heaven. Life towards death is always the gaping wound that is ever un-healing and already healed, but only through Christ. This work intends the poetic glimpse, the underlying liturgical beauty, the awe of silent prayer that permits us entrance into what appears as only exile.

Christ overcame death *through* his death, gave us paradise *through* death. He had to suffer and die to overcome it; he died to be resurrected.

That is why our living out the seven last words is a participation in the crucifixion as it is a participation in heaven. This saddest of all states brings us into the *poesis* of love, joy, and union in all its hard-won majesty. Each of us is already inside those seven last words in our protracted dying as both the experience of total abandonment—*why have you forsaken me*—and the gift of our immortality—*today you will be with me in paradise*. Neither experience expels the other. And this supremely high stakes poetry will be with us for the rest of our lives. It is the death sentence—the unquenchable *I thirst*—releasing us from death, *it is finished*! It is loss as loss—*they know not what they do*—while being gain—*behold your son, behold your mother*! Neither does the loss outwit the gain, nor does the gain undercut the loss on this side of eternity, so we too must *commend our spirits* to this salvific *poesis*, to the one Word made flesh.

In the seven last words, the nativity's Christ child is now liturgically, and in every unendurable sense of the literal, not too far removed to be recalled, but too near us, so tragically near that ours is his, that mine is thine. What an inheritance of impotence did our Christ take on to complete the distance that was ours to complete! The psalmist's words within the sheer poetic entanglement of humanity and God echo *almost* its length in space and time: "Why are you so far from helping me, and from the words of my roaring?" How can we forget that the Son, pinned to the dead tree of fallen ends and failed deeds, not only aged all the ages, with skin broken, faded, parched, and bones quaking beneath, but did so as the joy within the womb, as the child nourished on the breast, who laid near his mother's heart, a holy innocent ever cradled in her embrace. His thirst in dying is his thirst in the manger. How impossible this is, and yet truly the only thing needful. From cradle to cross, Christ becomes so profoundly our powerlessness, the interior and hidden poetry of our longing, of our inescapable dying, by becoming wholly the untranslated. In the seven last words, the beauty of the nativity is too near, the reality of love, as the total giving forth, is everything *because* it has pierced our sin so profoundly and entered its nothingness by means of abandonment. The only way is the way without power, becoming the surrender that prefigures all surrender, the *poesis* of the Word that descends and dies to save.

> This face, these hands and these feet, this side, this whole body speaks. It is itself a word we can hear in the silence. How does the Shroud speak? It speaks with blood, and blood is life! The Shroud is an Icon written in blood; the blood of a man who was scourged, crowned with thorns, crucified and whose right side

> was pierced. The Image impressed upon the Shroud is that of a dead man, but the blood speaks of his life. Every trace of blood speaks of love and of life. Especially that huge stain near his rib, made by the blood and water that flowed copiously from a great wound inflicted by the tip of a Roman spear. That blood and that water speak of life. It is like a spring that murmurs in the silence, and we can hear it, we can listen to it in the silence of Holy Saturday.
> —Pope Benedict XVI, "Veneration of the Holy Shroud"

Christ's love gifts us with the way through his wound, and the way *is* the wound, for Christ has risen with his scars. We receive salvation hiding in his wounds. What supreme poetry has he made his body, each wound is high and low poetry, "a spring that murmurs in the silence, and we can hear it, we can listen to it." This is the rosary of tears that begins in the memory of innocence and in the blood shared by all. My God, my God, I have no words to tell you. I have no reasons or logic or justification. The heart has reasons *beyond* reason. I lay down my longing into you. I give you my dying, which is my poetry, and you gave me yours. This is the exquisite armory made by your absence, the exquisite gift of being forsaken. The Christ child is simultaneously the crucified one, and will bear what we cannot, will give up the only ghost worthy to inhabit flesh and blood, for unless we be like this child, we cannot enter the kingdom of heaven.

His seven last words are the *untranslated* poetry that lays unspoken and unresolved in the center of each heart. He gives speech, sound, and an enduring *translated* word. Christ is *in* but not *of* the world. He overcomes the *in* and makes the world no longer *of* itself. He expands our souls to accommodate what is impossible and yet necessary to take-in: the wisdom of death's own wordless *poesis* recovered into life. Christ's last words are the invocation of this mystic translation within each of us which can unite us to others and to God even in the loneliness of death. For while we must make the final journey to God alone, and that finality is not suspended but a daily affair, we have the seven guideposts that make a friend to death. We can wrestle with death only to the point that death allows, it holds all the cards to the game of life. Death hints but refuses to allow us the completion of the untranslated. It never gives over its secret knowledge. We begin to receive its wisdom *only* as it puts us asleep, off to bed straightened out in pine box with sawdust faded from the sun. The sun shines because our moment is *already* a recollection, a past shot through time. We are one with death, beyond translation but not recognition. Christ speaks the Seven Last Words and we become His and He ours and we are finally the *poetry* of the Word.

We know not what we do—Christ is born to die. He becomes *of* the pine, *of* the stone, *of* the dust and can call out with us the consummate poetry of dying—*My God, why have you abandoned me*. He dies to become the translated Word between God and man. The Christ child was born to *thirst*, and Our Lady's heart was raised to break open and overflow with unbroken sorrow and joy—*today you will be with me in paradise*. She knows the meaning of the untranslated time which abides by the eternal—*for it is finished*. She can see the whole beauty and eternal transience of the moment which is all too much for us to navigate and understand, and we must—*commend the spirit*. Her child's heart is sheer love, it is everything, the immense and the little. In the Christ child, she sees the very birth-pangs of divinity and feels it throbbing in her heart—*behold your son, behold your mother*! Christ's existence connects the divine to the endlessly mortal heart, uniting the poetry of a human life, its protracted experience of dying, with the salvific Word.

> For the word of God is alive and active. Sharper than any double-edged sword, it penetrates even to dividing soul and spirit, joints, and marrow; it judges the thoughts and attitudes of the heart.
>
> —Hebrews 4:12

In this cycle of poetry, the overarching magnetizing force of finality is what draws out the meaning. The poets seek to remain wedded to that finality and to its paradoxical structure as the lodestar of all poetic speaking. It is impossible that Christ speaks that it is *finished*, it is impossible that we should be *forgiven*, and yet these two impossibilities are the reality of the seven last words. They are the total poetry of our renewed nature—*beholding* the other, beholding God as God beholds us. Christ so ardently *thirsts* to be loved by us that this thirst devours him. Before he *commends* his spirit, and before it is complete, he reveals the love of the mission through his thirst. Christ has chosen to be *abandoned* out of abundance, to be thirsty with and for us. In these last words, Christ holds the Word open for us to drink of its new life, its impossible love. When Christ thirsts—which will not end until we no longer sleep, until we have faces—he takes on the innumerable broken cisterns. Christ gives us his body and blood, which as infinite holds all love, all life, and all impossible goods made possible, his tabernacle is the unbroken cistern, the water of life, the *poesis* of the Word. He has commended his spirit and death is stripped of its end—*and we will be with him in paradise.*

> Any soul that drank the nectar of your passion was lifted.
> From that water of life he is in a state of elation.
> Death came, smelled me, and sensed your fragrance instead.
> From then on, death lost all hope of me.
> —Rumi, "Any Soul That Drank the Nectar"

Christ's seven last words have given us sight through his dying, given us the words through his word. We are powerless alone to fulfill the inner desire of all poetic speaking: the power to create. But Christ has given us that power, to make what fails be the *poesis* of paradise. Through his body and blood, we are given the poetry of the untranslated, the Word beneath and exceeding all image and likeness. Our broken beings, let them fall apart, for they need to break if we are to be near him. And as we break, we are taught the *poesis* of the eternal, for Christ is not words in time but the Word of time, configuring all experience. Christ has given us immortal life not by denying death but by permitting us to go into death, to live in death—which is the threshold of all poetry—to be at the heart of death. The seven last words are not an abstract living in the idea of God, for that was not enough for our covetous longing hearts. We desired the freedom that creatures cannot express, one that breaks the maxims and standards and enters the ultimate of each untranslated human and divine bond. The last words speak the poetry of the impossible and the true, they speak to each of us as if each is the sole inheritor of the universe, as if each word was meant for us alone. That is the goal of all good poetry—to pierce the veil: to speak what lays mute yet relentlessly pressing at the center of our locked up dying hearts. Christ dies so that the pure poetry is spoken, the veil is pierced and torn. Christ is the infinitely inventive and infinitely creative *poet/poesis*. The extent of his love for us was found when he took on abandonment so that we could become teachable, so that we could bear the full mark of divine love. In him we too take on what is untranslatable and survive the inner dynamite of all true poetry, which occurs in dying and can never be spoken or shared. Christ's flesh and blood is a tasted fragrance, the poetry of the eternally dying, eternally living Word.

Christ is the poet of all poets. In his seven last words he took the stone of our hearts and transformed them, in sweetest alchemy, into the softness of flesh and blood capable of eternal happiness, capable of speaking the paradisal words. He gave us, not the image of goodness, nor likenesses in beauty, nor the perceptions of truths, nor even the participation in immortality, but a full partnership in eternal life, where I can love God with the pure *poetry/poesis* that admits no lacking.

> The nightingale with drops of his heart's blood
> Had nourished the red rose, then came a wind,
> And catching at the boughs in envious mood,
> A hundred thorns about his heart entwined.
> Like to the parrot crunching sugar, good
> Seemed the world to me who could not stay
> The wind of Death that swept my hopes away.
> —Hafez, "The Nightengale"

On the Love of Miscellaneous Things

> The most beautiful arrangement is a pile of things poured out at random.
> —Heraclitus

The poems are organized by each of the seven last words as ultimate passage into the human experience of our beings magnetized by finality. The poets stand in the tide of change but are also moving images of eternity drawn in every beginning, in every experience, in every half-waking thought towards the irresistible pole of the last things. The effort is not linguistically to *put on* finality, or to gain the objectival perspective to speak *about* the terminus, or to set up a sort of spectatorial distance by which we see the vista of the end, but to let the experience that penetrates our vision, and crucifies our bodies in age and endurance, wash over us with the words of Christ. What results may not so much be overtly thematic but more thematizing, not subject but person, not category, topic, concept, but locus, home, and even nomadic homelessness.

These cycles of poetry, for better or for worse, for loss or for gain, seek to avoid the easily won unity achieved by the mind. The miscellany of the work is a guard against the temptation for an untimely unity. Only a unity that is timely—one that understands that if there are beings there is a *way* for beings to be—can unify the heart in Truth, Goodness, and Beauty. Our own dying in the face or facelessness of the ultimate, and the impossible but necessary astonishment of the dying God, yokes us from the achieved pseudo-harmonies that posit the human person as center of the universe. As we walk with Christ during the stations of the cross, so that thought *serves* Being, this poetry cycle is an *inlaying* of our words imbedded in the Word. It seeks a submersion into the delectation, anguish, thirst, neediness, ecstasy, and the Mamertine surrender of Christ's ultimate poetry. While the inclination to a systematic unity where we speak about each of the seven last words may well be a natural one, it would fail to be *of* and *in* the poetry of the Word. Because the words themselves are the supreme *poesis* of the last things, the eschaton, they are best laid bare in non-mediated poetry that may fall short but nevertheless falls *within* the givenness of Christ's radical surrender of divine and human transposition. We *are* forgiven, paradisal, beheld, forsaken, thirsting, finished, commended.

The task at hand is to rediscover by embodiment the creativity and play that is always the sanctifying groundwork for the dark nights of the soul. The joys of beatitude are discovered in a miscellany of intruding life. Ecstasy, suffering, penance, and death surprise us in the bypassed and the overlooked experiences, in the places and people we least expect. For Christ, the first shall the last and the last shall be the first, so too must our poetry take heed, not neglecting the little things that cling in corners. The poets are magnetized and drawn without resistance to Christ's poetry in the seven last words and what may come must come. We seek the felt experience of the *forgiven*; the crystalline waters of the *paradisal*; the azure penetrative gaze of being *beheld*, the blood-cleaving thorns of the *forsaken*; the panting deer *thirsting*; the exacting knowledge that it is finally *finished*. In all of this, our souls are our bodies, and our bodies are our souls *commended* over to God.

When reflection peers too dismissively, discarding the miscellaneous as extraneous and accidental, it begins to view not only the world but God as deterministic and often competitive with the world. God becoming human—child especially—throws that view overboard. We too must follow suit going headlong into the abyss. This *poesis* preceding the ideational systematic may be loss, we may lose ourselves in the miscellany, or it may be exactly how the glimpse of heaven itself is given to us. What the child at play has is what our poetry in Christ seeks to rediscover. We became thinkers only after we had ruined ourselves as knowers. So much of life is a rootless demand for self-imposed meaning, unity, order. Christ's seven last words as the poetry of all poetry, and Christ the poet of all poets, chasten us. Until we become like this child and recover the love of the miscellaneous—of the little things that appear fragmentary and insignificant to eyes that cannot or will not see—we cannot enter the kingdom of heaven. Even in the graveyard, it is the radical miscellany that evokes the prayer of the observer.

> All souls of children taken as they slept
> Are your companions, partners of your ease,
> And the green souls of all these autumn trees
> Are with you through the silent spaces swept.
> Your virgin body gave its gentle breath
> Untainted to the gods. Why should we grieve,
> But that we merit not your holy death?
> —George Santayana, "For W.P."

The world is too full of Christ's sacrifice, so much so that it is the unavoidable mystery. His *poesis* is not in a straight line of deterministic cause and effects but all the loving miscellany of a life well lived from the lilies of the field to the hidden chapel found at the edge of overgrown woods. It is this miscellany as directionality that ensures freedom and does not close us off to freedom, to the gift, and to transcendence. The organization of the poems into each of the seven last words is not to liberate the miscellaneous experience into a forced theme but to unveil how our experiential walking with Christ's *poetry*—his dying and eternal life—is always innermost in each of us. Because of this, Christ alone can offer each of us sole inheritance of the universe.

A Brief Word on Art

> The Beauty of God is the Being of all that is.
> —St. Thomas Aquinas, *Commentary on the Divine Names*

> Dostoyevsky once let drop the enigmatic phrase: "Beauty will save the world." What does this mean? For a long time it used to seem to me that this was a mere phrase. Just how could such a thing be possible? When had it ever happened in the bloodthirsty course of history that beauty had saved anyone from anything? Beauty had provided embellishment certainly, given uplift—but whom had it ever saved?
> —Alexander Solzhenitsyn, Nobel Prize lecture

If that first and often lasting invitation into faith—not faith in general but *this* faith and *this* person, Christ—is given to us *through* Beauty, it is the monumental task of the artist to help us experience the Beautiful, to recover Beauty in our lives. The transcendentally Beautiful is always another diamond facet of the Good and the True. Art crucially opens the door to Goodness, Truth, and to the faith that nowadays is much restricted, derided, and closed off. Beauty may save the world. Each of the cycles of poems pertaining to the seven last words will be accompanied by art by my co-author, the artist Carol Scott. Here, the unabashedly Beautiful reanimates those lost wells of experience so that we can, once again, *feel* the poetizing Word enfleshed, Word made flesh, the Word of our flesh human and divine.

Each piece of art in the book is selected to evoke the miscellany of a life lived towards the supernatural, not as mere abstraction but as an incarnate ecstasy. This miscellany means the freedom of being given to creatures so that they may love magnificently or fail as Icarus fallen. In the selected art, the miscellany cannot and will not be overtly systematized to the point that meaning becomes meaning-giver and paradoxically loses meaning! As a response, the mystery of the human soul and body, as entwined miscellany and play, is situated and symbolized in sheer brilliant color and form. Each canvas is one compressed image, unveiling the human person as marbled Galatea carved by *eros* into living presence. They are poetizing glimpses of the reality that the body *is* the soul as the soul *is* the body. This enjoining of poles, body and soul, color and form, into seamless robe, places the human person on the horizon between time and eternity, the lowest of spiritual substances and the highest of carnal beings. The artist undresses the audacity, indeed the magic of our creative life. She unsheathes light and reflection and saturates forms in the enigmatic resonances of light and reflection, shadow and vision, of a recollection that desires to re-collect *Being* itself. In these images we recover the forever numinous and intensifying invitation to Christ's ultimate poem—his flesh and blood, his body and soul, the God and the man—grafted to his seven last words. Every image is as rain: it washes clean and overwhelms us by changing reflection. We peer from a different angle and yet the only one that saves, giving us the strange sense of looking down at the skies:

> And indeed this is the last and not the least gracious of the casual works of magic wrought by rain: that while it decreases light, yet it doubles it. If it dims the sky, it brightens the earth. It

gives the roads (to the sympathetic eye) something of the beauty of Venice. Shallow lakes of water reiterate every detail of earth and sky; we dwell in a double universe. Sometimes walking upon bare and lustrous pavements, wet under numerous lamps, a man seems a black blot on all that golden looking-glass, and could fancy he was flying in a yellow sky. But wherever trees and towns hang head downwards in a pigmy puddle, the sense of Celestial topsy-turvydom is the same. This bright, wet, dazzling confusion of shape and shadow, of reality and reflection, will appeal strongly to any one with the transcendental instinct about this dreamy and dual life of ours. It will always give a man the strange sense of looking down at the skies.

—G. K. Chesterton, *A Miscellany of Men*

All great artists experience the passionate *ecstasis*—the in-the-body and out-of-body longing for God who calls us through vision beyond vision. Here we are reminded of the power of art and Beauty in Endo's great novel *Silence*. The art is a simple carved image of Christ used to ferret out believers. If you trampled on the image, you prove you are not a believer and spared death. Our character in the novel denied Christ, but the art *forever* remained in his soul, "like a spring that murmurs in the silence, and we can hear it, we can listen to it in the silence." The Beauty endured and persisted, perfused his heart and saved him, becoming the poetry of the last things. With Dostoevsky, it can save the world:

> I, too, stood on the sacred image. For a moment this foot was on his face. It was on the face of the man who has been ever in my thoughts, on the face that was before me on the mountains, in my wanderings, in prison, on the best and most beautiful face that any man can ever know, on the face of him whom I have always longed to love. Even now that face is looking at me with eyes of pity from the plaque rubbed flat by many feet. "Trample!" said those compassionate eyes. "Trample! Your foot suffers in pain; it must suffer like all the feet that have stepped on this plaque. But that pain alone is enough. I understand your pain and your suffering. It is for that reason that I am here." "Lord, I resented your silence." "I was not silent. I suffered beside you."

—Shūsaku Endō, *The Silence*

This work is designed to be read alongside *All This and Heaven Too: A Guide for All Souls* and *The Impossible Possibility: Christ and the Problems of Forgiveness* (Cascade, 2024) where several poems in this volume begin the chapters of these books. Read in unison, these works elicit a recovery of the hope for heaven and for the resurrected life in a readable and inviting form. The poetic and artistic emphases envision a real and robust view of heaven. Paradise is won through the passion, though depths of joy, love, finitude, and suffering, and not the well-meaning but often empty sense of the "better-place," which is disembodied, uninviting, and has lost its holy mystique. To rediscover the magnetizing pull of the last words is to feel and desire the great challenge and gift of the first Commandment:

> *"Love the Lord your God with all your heart, and with all your soul, and with all your mind."*

You Intoxicate My Soul, by Carol Scott

Foreword

THE MIDST OF TODAY is saturated, because fed by the dull, flat fatigue of apathy with its engineered distractions, clever designs of consumption that endlessly collaborate with the rapacious devouring of what lies before us, especially as it lies within; making sure that all goes unnoticed. A concatenation of scheming prophylactics ensures our near-global myopia, an enabling destructive sedation. Here, harnessing the last seven words of Christ as a meta-framework, this work, wielding intertwined words and images of profound and exquisite persuasion, returns reality to us. That which is brought back, which never left, but was forgotten, summoned so very beautifully in these pages is of such welcoming vertigo, the genius of which is its indigenous murmur, like a lost shadow. There is no novelty here, no contrived tricks, but rather the miracle of the ignored, now remembered, restored. Throughout, attention is arrested, and rearrested, set free to think, and to think again. Allowed to rest, to sleep, only in the bosom of a night that lies within the abyss of a promise kept, made, and arriving. Gilson and Scott's work is one utterly necessary for our time, if we are to live it at all, if we are to have time, for they bring back the gift of eternity, and its earthly, natural desire. My gratitude for this work is utter.

    Conor Cunningham
    University of Nottingham

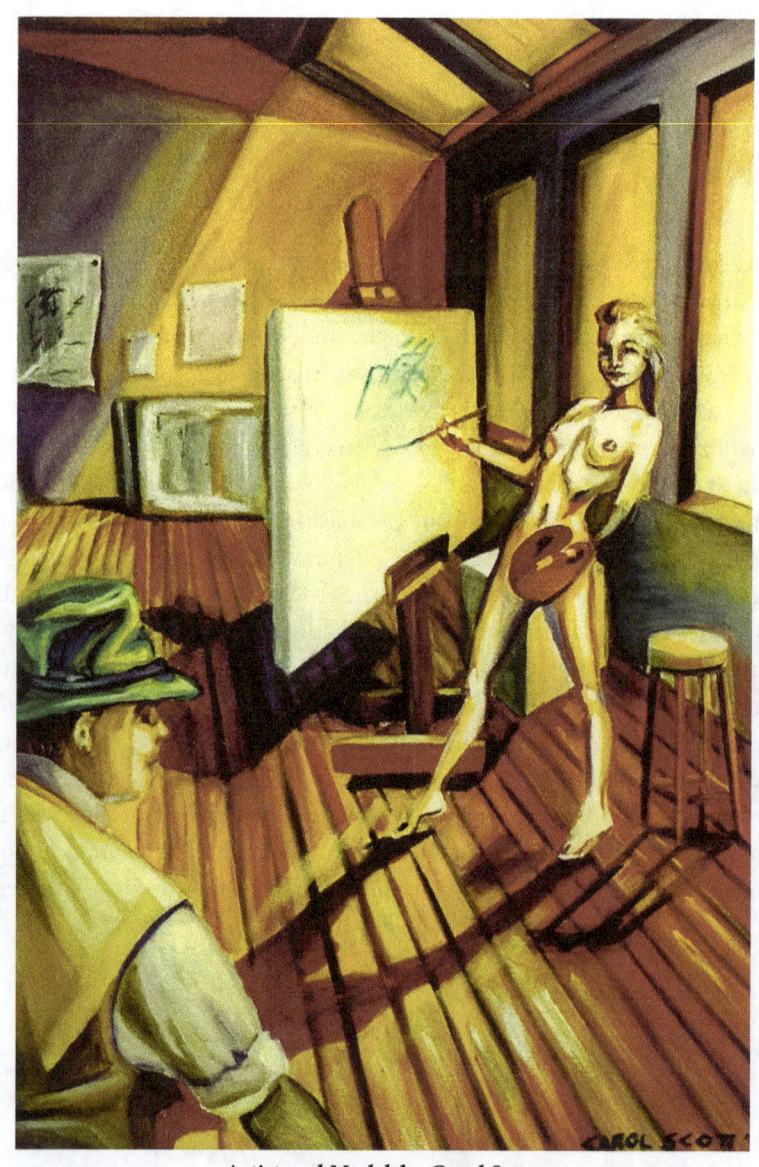

Artist and Model, by Carol Scott

Acknowledgments

CAROL AND I WOULD like to thank Conor Cunningham, especially for his generous and beautiful reflections in the foreword. We would also like to thank Matthew Levering, Margaret McCarthy, and Jennifer Newsome Martin for their astute attentiveness, intellectual and spiritual rigor, and care towards this project.

Many thanks to the brilliant, engaging, and generous editorial team at Wipf & Stock. Most particularly, Michael Thomson, Matthew Wimer, Zechariah Mickel, Jonathan Hill, Mike Surber and especially Robin Parry, our editor, whose gifts of vision and style raise the quality of the work and do so with much love and care.

Thank you to the exceptional and welcoming intellectual and spiritual community at St. Vincent de Paul Regional Seminary.

To our dearest comet of a friend, Susie, our Ursus Minor!

Deeply grateful for Cyril, Connie, Fr. Labastida, Joseph, Bianca, St. Francis College NY, and the community at St. Vincent de Paul Regional Seminary.

Most appreciative of the collectors who have valued and collected the artwork.

For our families—all love, and all time.

Hear No Evil, by Carol Scott

I

Father Forgive Them, They Know Not What They Do

When our eyes met in the compartment our spiritual fortitude deserted us both; I took her in my arms, she pressed her face to my breast, and tears flowed from her eyes. Kissing her face, her shoulders, her hands wet with tears—oh, how unhappy we were!—I confessed my love for her, and with a burning pain in my heart I realized how unnecessary, how petty, and how deceptive all that had hindered us from loving was. I understood that when you love you must either, in your reasonings about that love, start from what is highest, from what is more important than happiness or unhappiness, sin or virtue in their accepted meaning, or you must not reason at all.

—Anton Chekhov, *About Love*

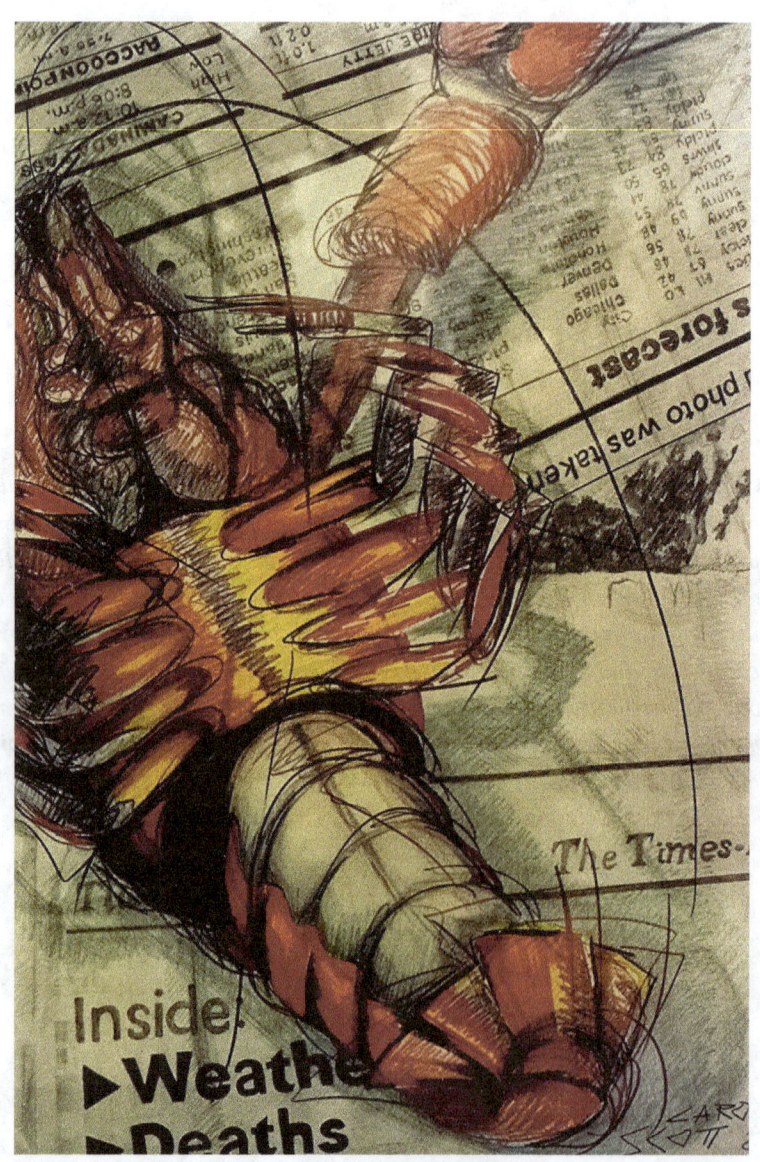
Obituary Crawfish, **by Carol Scott**

There Are Stories Older than Sin

There are stories older than sin
Older than the single material life
That sacrificed itself
Becoming the many

I have forgotten how to sleep
What it means
To surrender my eyes
To end the circulating sight
Last engine
Lighting the cirque

I have misplaced the seasons
The petals that fall
They are not snow
Not the leaves
The water's edge
Uncollected noise
Static of the mechanical heart
Humming through deep space

The mind perishes nightly
Into stories untarnished by thought
Stories before the sun
Stories that brought
The moon to existence

The height of the satellite
Is the depth of my waking
I have forgotten that nighttime
Is made of dreaming
The vision of you downing me

Somewhere in this lonely causation
Planetary rivers and streams
Guides and guidebooks
Paths scarring the land
I am white stone cleaving the green

You perish nightly into echo
In the land of always
Not timeless
But *always* time
Forever time
For time must move
Till your reach is mine
Into the stalks of sugarcane
The earth will be watered
With our time someday

Star-sucked lover
Wild ageless silken lover
Lover of mine
Body logic of midnights and purples
And things that crush and coo
Teach me to sleep
I forget everything but you

I have come for the dipped
Underside of your knee
Where mysteries are made

Exhaled lands and seas
If only death were a packaged dream

My Secret

I sense in the late nights
I am not long for this world
The instinctual refrain ages
The way the body changes
My sight has already failed
In different ways

I can still close my eyes
And see you as you were
But I lost something today
Decades of one thing
Not long left
This emblemed silver
That wound me into you
I lost the weight of it
As I tap the table
The way the heat and the cold
Changed the ring

Sometimes I know
I am not long for this place
The person of my body
This world
Other times I may live forever
But my eyes have a memory to them
They chase the night as last call

Last drink
Last things

I do not see very well
I do not know if I am looking at you
But I can close my eyes
And see you
The day we made love on the floor
Long words of your silver
Written across my body
They are always there
Press my skin and you can feel them
Suspended

Sometimes the mind
Scatters the dust
I think of poured syrup
The joys you knew
All of it a jar of compressed maple
It has a scent to me these years
You linger as fresh soap
Clean
A keen innocence
Wafting in pain
I could never take your tears

I have never walked in deep forest
It frightens me
I can run the city blocks in rain
I know I am not long for this world
I imagine the leaves give way
To some hidden depth
I do not want you to go

Do not bury me in the forest far away
Let me be sugar and light and morning
To live forever
I think I will live forever
Sometimes though I know
My time is gone

I lost something precious today
A token
A remnant of floors and sights
So many insights of the mind
Scanning the emptied earth
A locket of eternal life

God
I love that you have lived and breathed
Break me all over again

The Mind of the Beloved

Your conscience
Footfall in snow
Compressed
Crystal white
Under shadowless moonlight

I need your peerless curved singular feature
Pressed into form
Tread across my land
Infinite mind living inside
This marooned need

Forgive me
Forgive this body and this mind
Forgive these thoughts
These things
Falling open exposed without cover
Your foolish lover
All matter and form crushed
Circulating the tear of instant ice

I will know all earths touched by you
I will bow at your shadows in play
If only you were endless day
My soul

My soul
If only the grace of your need

You dip into my snow
Carving transferring shape
Your waveless light tapers
The passageway of spliced lines
This trading of minds
Forgive me
All fire and love
All matter and form crushed
Circulating the tear of instant ice

Felix Culpa

When you close your eyes
You have all the power
To break my body out of my soul
Transported
Between eighty-eight keys
Ten million colors
A universe fourteen billion years old

How can one person be everything?

The universe cannot go on
Hurling itself until it dies
This cataclysm
Will steal all life

It took twelve years for Michelangelo
To create the Rondanini
He carved till he died
Cut away the marble
Nothing remained
Except an armless Christ

How can one person be everything?

Every second we live
Numberless drops of blood

Till the moment of death
We keep reproducing ourselves
Galaxies of age
Three hundred thousand light years
Wrapped diameter
Miles of lives before us
Boundless ossuary under the earth
What can it mean?

How can one person be everything?

Infinite gaping mouth
Endless space
Impossible to calculate
When I lose myself
Cast me low
To live under the water
Where all dead go to live again
Thrown net
Knot after knot of heavy rope
Catching and sinking

How can one person be everything?

Corpus Christi

Burned knees rocking back and forth
Burying the flesh in fiber
Downing the old Adam

Everlasting bruising kiss
Fire of the fire
Lips smoldering you

Dipped magnetic arch
Flexing estuary of molten steel
Cupped bone overflow
Muscled ache
Your rising shadow interlocked

Everlasting blushing touch
Wine of the wine
Lips somersaulting you

Body of Christ
Punctuated razed sky
The air descending
The animal cry

Body of Christ
Quaked divided sigh

The parting earth
The hawk in flight

Body of Christ
Moonless gravity
The rising tide
The end of the honeybee

Your Soul
The eye of Providence
The foxhole in battle
Three-winged dragonfly
The grace of last prayer

Amare

The cruel cuts through
A practiced blade
Already prepared way
Loveless pantomimes
Dying inside stone

But I get to love the good of you

Frozen pulse we cannot feel
The serpent at the clutched heel
Splicing the life
Unthawed block of ice
Freezing to death

But I get to love the warmth of you

This is the dark wood
The place of thorn
Uncreative treason
Dressed in nonsense
Weighted seamless gown

But I get to love the soul of you

The eaten sin kills
Long before we die

Fools piloting ships of fools
But I have known you
Unconfessed roses rendered
The house of the Good
The only way through

I get to love the love of you

Pouring Out

We cannot give life
You receive me
As I receive you

Whatever you want
Whatever you need
What ocean should I drink?

This infinite league
Poured out unconquered need
Contracting with your touch

You interiorize the plead
All oil and drawn spice
Beggar at your parted knee
Transmuted in hot gold
Breaking the law of diminishing returns

Such honey from the marrow
Bright red burying kiss in soft passage
Poured out hallowed ground
Every endgame ends in you

Whatever you want
What earth can I move?
What heaven can I shake?

Invisible magnet
Event of missing you
We are born in time
Creatures of need

But God you came close
You came close
When you opened me
Breaking the law of entropy

If I could love you more
I would burn the earth
Whatever you want
Whatever you need
What ocean should I drink?

If tomorrow is not tomorrow
If tomorrow I crash and burn
If tomorrow I know the earth
If tomorrow I lose my thought
My walk, my being
God, you came close
You are the water
The lover's head
The opening

Need

This need
Giving it all till morning
Give and take
Shaken wild need
Descending fjord
Glacial drink

This need
Mansions of your body
Marbled columns
Architectural planes
Seas of golden vessels
Ascending deed

I am the sigh
The swift sigh
The long sigh
Reading your wants
The body of me
Soaked clutched body need

This need
Sculpted pink tourmaline
Uncased speaking
Kerosene risen knee
Roping the moon to the floor

Pared down apple core
Filled out body need

I am the sigh
The swift sigh
The long sigh
Reading your wants
The body of me
Soaked clutched body need

Broken Down

The founding form
Spliced infinite magenta
Separated and broken
The terrible alone

Magnetizing quarters
Phantom dividing lines
Split open
In trails of lust

Black shined anchor
Caught on the latch
Pulling the ship down
Disassembled in leagues
Below the sea

Unconquered shade
Unattended sensation
Sold images without relation
The terrible alone

Poisoned nectar
Heart of calcified bone
Evacuated treasure chest
In trails of lust

Pooling ledge
Tensile metric
Shivering in nudity
Faded blushing cusp
Below the sea

This is eternal loss
Foreclosed sight
Instantiations of the Cross
If only there was life

If Only

If I were floating above the earth
Seeing only masses of blue and white
If I were clothed in coldness
And vast emptiness
I would be ready to die

All the same
I am swimming against the inevitable
Too far to make it home
It would be too far

You see
I desire to be far away from the world
Far away from those who govern it
To live more and to disintegrate too

Sometimes it is all too much
The way houses are made
The way the walls
Cover the sad specimens of time
Layers of trespassed space and history
Impenetrable foundations

If only they were shallower
Unaware, less resistance
If only this house was built on sand

It would collapse with ease
I would watch what is mine implode
As fires keep warm these things
Past forgetting
If only the foundations
Were not as deep
Ancient below the earth
So very long ago

Walls are made of layers
Layers of insulation
You see some part of me
Lays in the bed of the earth
And still I am stranded
In the airless black
Looking down at the air
The oxygen I cannot breathe
The land peering into my body

It is always one or the other
Motioning canopy swimming body
But the distance is too far
Too far
I will not make it in time

If only the foundations were weak
If only my soul was built on shifting sands
And things fell apart easier quicker
Things from things
Dissolving without pain

If only your kiss and hold
The house of my body
Motioning in the void

I have felt the softness
Of your face on mine
Oh I would melt without pain

God of Fools

You fool I know you, God
I know you have a plan
But I am not willing to remain steady and see the joy
Even if I do know there is joy to come
There is always joy to come with you

I need you to suffer
I will never hurt another except you
Your foolish love is the grave
I desire your sting and weeping
More than my blood and kiss
A confused grace a waste

You love me in ways that drown oceans
I have no desire to survive
You will love the loss of me
All that insignificance
Significant only to you
What a fool you are
Wailing in airless space

You are all good
All cruelty and all love
I cannot love what I do not know
But you made yourself known
weeping for me as I refuse you

Foolish one
Keeping me to the end and there is an end
I know that too

Fool of all fools but I know you
All love
All protracted honey
All inscrutable good

My terrorizing fool too good
Too much grace and too much joy
I can refuse it laced with wine and bitterness
your exquisite pain
Forgotten to all

My loss is all insignificance
That is your great lesson and I have learned it well
Made in your image

I will not give to you even as I do not doubt
You are vision made of love
A fool
I can refuse you
I will give you nothing other than I am
God of fools

What can you do?
Take my child my home my love my life
Yet you are all good
What can you do?
You have taken everything and still I can refuse you to the end
Remind me dear absent one
Who is the fool?

The Metaphysics of Love

To the One Whom I Desire . . .

For all his gentleness and humility born flesh and blood
He descended as Star hurling through the cosmos
Stretched out Corpus Christi, knotted wood of my sighing

To My One Heart-Splitting All . . .

It is a terrible power to destroy love
This is the Sin before any one evil
The mystery of the gulf laced on lips
Wreckages we cannot find
Misplaced life, dying time
Death of our bodies
Death of our kind

To My Body Towed through Weeping Glass for You . . .

We are fixed to die burning away
Hidden one
We played the universe
Held all the cards and lost

I love you with the kind of mad love
That unites the living and the dead
Understand

I would turn the world upside down
To tell you the things I cannot know

To My Hidden Lover Eclipsing Me, Eden of Lapped Citrus and Wildflowers . . .

Hell is no place, but it is time
Unrealized without his death
Illusion in our power
The more as the lesser
Fossil of the living

To You the Undressed Contours of My Mind . . .

What I do know is that if we lose out in every sense of the word
We are no longer persons
Persons make places
You make places
I think of your home, your home
To be home with you
Loving you
But hell is the loss of place
The more in hell every love erased

To Your Soundless Eyes Looking for Me . . .

Christ's love for you will rupture the remaining quarters of your heart
Rape the thorn from the vine
I am all temptation bound up in what I cannot do
I need to love you with that reach and deep
But I cannot encompass this leap
His loving dying for you it will make you weep
Your bones rattle
To feel you, to feel you at home again

Quaking with each tear

To Your Skin Smoother Than Pages Turned with Lips . . .

The dead do not bury the dead
The dust cannot reanimate
Swept into floods
Submerged brutal last and only choice
Worthless tools blown apart
Thirty pieces every time we lie
The only power left was suffering unto death
Into the placeless end
Caught in ice where the soul learns to die

I love you with the kind of mad love
That unites the living and the dead
Understand
I would turn the world upside down
To tell you the things I cannot know

To My Compressed Passion Shaped in Your Clay . . .

The leaves scatter on the ground
Red and brown dirt and clay
More than physical dying, more than decomposition
Our bodies
Another sort of scattering
We barely glimpse the fearful rupture in space and time
Before the spirits fell they mirrored eternity
When angels refuse their image, the earth is lashed and cleaved apart
A comet hurling across history into bloodless nothingness
Our blood to come

To You Firewater Water of Life, Shallow Curve That Breathes My Everywhere . . .

Angels are falling everywhere we walk and breathe
I hold you and you hold me
And still they fall
Before time
After time
As time
Their very beings have no end no corporeality
The fallen spirits take up the earth and take up the ether
God un-relinquishing
If only I were with you loving you
How could they lose themselves in terrible departing
If only I were with you loving you

To You Fruit of the Stone, Substance of My Tears, Gathering of You Gathering Me . . .

This tear in the fabric before the altar of our blood
Becomes the spilt exile, drenched bitter gall
In Eden before our fall
The fallen angel lost it all
We are closer to angels than this animalesque
Once ageless bodies
Violent separated soul

To Finding You One Millimeter below My Skin, Your lightest Touch an Ocean . . .

Your body is your soul
Your soul is bound body
Seamless cloth
Hurling comet broke open universe

Plummeting away
If only I were with you held into near heaven
Loving you
Your body wound around mine
We would not know their fallenness
The gaping wound
If only I were home
All of you
The substance of home
Without his dying on the Cross
The enfleshed soul cleaved apart
I dream of home, your home

I love you with the kind of mad love
That unites the living and the dead
Understand
I would turn the world upside down
To tell you the things I cannot know

To You Sheltered in Perfect Sleeping above All Storm, Tongued Waterfall Dreaming for Me . . .

Our souls are comets descending into the abyss
Second death, death of the soul
For beings made not to die
We are drowning in the lie
Only God can survive this fall of all falls
These wounds of Christ
Place your finger in his side
Hell overcoming hell
For whom the bell tolls

To the One Made of Honey and Incense I Drink as Wine Remaining Me . . .

Christ suffered more than world and universe
He made death the portal, the dress rehearsal
The end of ways and means
A no way, the once dead end
When I die I will see you again
Christ is this rescue mission
When we sleep and when we wake
Risen body with his scars

To Your Hidden Cord Binding Me, Alleviating Time . . .

I love you to the end of matter
To the ends Christ traversed
Crossed abyss made life
I will cross it forever for you
Loving you madly
The Christ in you
In all my living and dying
I long for the earth and for the sunshine of you
The waters that flow from Christ's side
Kiss of the dew
Your home, your home

I love you with the kind of mad love
That unites the living and the dead
Understand
I would turn the world upside down
To tell you the things I cannot know

Forgive: The Shared Poems of Artist Carol Scott & Caitlin Smith Gilson

Material Desire, by Carol Scott

Reverie in Four Parts

I. Reverie

All the roses
That cover my memory
Collect and take me into them

What does this mean
But that I am drifting
In and out of reverie

Flooded seas at the doorstep of your body
A boat of incense rowed beneath the tidal moon
You
Buried waves
Burned in effigy

Petals textured and colors
Descending from the mist
All things
Studied ecstasy
This

If these were the last days of my life
They were happy ones
All texture and color
You
Rowed beneath me

II. Intensity

I sense your fragrance
Smoke
Liquid lounging
Indulging the individual

Cooled cavorting intensities
Winter's cologne
Empress gin
Mixed in alchemic blue

Do not let the crown of thorns
Prick my brain
Nuisance nightmare
Collective travel
Hold on
Tighten your claw
Studied in ecstasy

No umbrella can protect
This deluge destroys dreams
Wake up
Come back to me

III. Desire

There are only so many hours in the day
That can be filled with ache for you
With joy for your voice
Descending ship
Into the whirlpool

Life again
Lanced perfection
The rain around your skin
Bolts of sapphire silk and coral sun
Your profile highlighted in the wet streets
Which take on and take in reflection

There are only so many interwoven seconds
Until they are left behind
Transfixed into minutes and hours
A transfusion of anchored time
Plunging to the seabed
Sunk into the need for you

IV. Time

Life cannot fit this box
Desire does not follow the clock
Death is not timely
Love is clay
Infinitely bending to fit the other
An invitation to smile
Energy rushing exploding into exaltation
Dying
Eyes that read you
Touch that sees you
What can I do?
Time in the world takes time from you

Tossed Alive

I am in the center of irresistible waves
Chilled wild light
Breathing the God before there was Cross
The ancient power fatal force
Moving all blood to the center
Pumping furiously to my extremities

The current has pulled me farther beyond the beachhead
Tossed alive
This immemorial uncurbed wheel of life

I sight my skin beneath the waves
Glimmering
Almost to the surface
White of dying
White of new life
The movement of the green before it rises
Riots of white
Cut glass
Then sheen immersion
Breathing the God before there was Cross

You are at this moment
Stamped into me before thought
For the split second
Your image

Bears another force
Moving all blood to my center
Tossed alive

Touching your body is creation
A final creation touched
House of your body
You
Image of all images

I am time-centered with an immortal Cross
How can I think of an age before Christ?
What thought of beginning?
What thought of end?

Ceaseless circles
Bodies closer to the end
Standing inside the self
Hastening

Take me where the white caps break
Pulled down under the ocean
Schooled in life
Imbibe this soul

All the paragliders are landing
Fabric swiftly collapsing
How can we help the other?
Crossing paths to infinity
Waving rhythmic push
Working ways
Finding God

All Your Light on Me

I love the sunshine
It could be that my hair
Is made of some ancient form
Of its burnt-out dust
And as the sun
Becoming gentler
Lighter
Softer in you
I am missing you
It is settling in
The ache

Even in the morning
When I do not wish to wake
I feel the life of the sun
The shining presence unmoved by time
The sun moves unspent bodies
Into unspoken grace
Haunted by the whole reality
You are eclipse itself
Hovering over my senses

I miss the atmosphere
The way you caress the sunlight
How it pours off your skin
My long gold draping your back

This contrast is the all-loving
Slide of my lips taking you in
Squeezed citrus crisp fall
Time of our past
Time recalled
I am missing you
It is settling in
The ache

My soul stretches back
Knotted up in your kisses as sunshine
Dreaming our bodies
Your skin
Glowing in all seasons
Brought into reason
The double ache of you eclipsing me
I will dream of the food of your soul
The food of your body dreaming mine

I have felt sunset the day one dies
When it is done
But you eclipse the sun

I am coming home
To watch the sun move over you
In one long unbroken day

I wish the night remained the night
My hair falling on your body
My life flowing into you
The double ache of you eclipsing me

Shadows dancing in the dark
It was only a moment ago

Of exquisite joy manifested love

Gold turns to yellow roses
With fragrant blooms
Petals falling on and on

There are many bodies
But yours is the only one that holds your soul
My soul
I pray for the moments yet to come
I remember

To Whom Do I Say Goodnight?

To whom do I say goodnight?
When you are not in my arms
Come to me even as phantom
End this feeling of loneliness
No lullaby for lovers

It has been since the last moon
Robbed sight of the stars that I slept
Then I could think of you in peace

If the stars would return
My breathing would be your form
If the moon would share the stars
Your shape
Then my spirit too would wander home
These things immaterial have their weight
They lead me
Soft pull of the earth
To your earth
Hunting for sleep

I pray it is night this night
And dream into the earth
I pray it is night this night
The fairyland of you
Become the real once again

The sense of you is circulation
Fevered waking
Your touch claims the universe

I never had the earth
I had it with you

Dreams of you are love's whispers
Somewhere between fantasy and memory
Night's prophecy and daylight's reality
Happy in the womb
Beautiful love
Piked highest and unbound
I will be with you
No more dreaming

You never had the earth
You had it with me

Forgive Me Love

Forgive me love
It has been hard
But I love you and adore you

I think of you in rain and sunshine
All because of how the glass weathers the storm
How the windows let in the light
As if nothing other than light ever existed
And this one comprising reality shines only through you
An everlasting day made of your grace and glory

Anything makes me think of you
Say *land* and it is you
Say *blue* and it is you
If the stones of the church should crumble
Tumble in two
You could put them back together
I know it to be true

You are the bells and the choir
The words and said prayer
The candle wax and the incense
My body clothed when it is bared
Your arms do to me
I never want to leave
Say *night* and it is you

Say *thread* and it is you
For we are linked by powers more than time
We will be the end of the other
And the beginning of ourselves

It has been hard days lover
But you are the sun and heaven above
All things are the thinking of you

Your soft quiet voice
Soothes my troubled soul
I cry like a baby struggling to hope
Replace the *whys* of despair
I will not be crucified
I will rise with Christ
Let every color of the rainbow overflow my eyes

The power of us
The magnitude of moments
Everything makes me think of you
Life becoming art
Genius of the heart
Your beauty never disguised
You are the vision and the visionary
You will write and write some more
All things are the thinking of you

11

Today You Will Be with Me in Paradise

Sometimes, when I've thought of my life, and the little pleasure I've had in it, I've believed that, maybe, I was one of those doomed to die by the falling of a star from heaven; "And the name of the star is called Wormwood; and the third part of the waters became wormwood; and men died of the waters, because they were made bitter." One can bear pain and sorrow better if one thinks it has been prophesied long before for one: somehow, then it seems as if my pain was needed for the fulfilment; otherwise it seems all sent for nothing.

—Elizabeth Gaskill, *North and South*

North Star, **by Carol Scott**

I Know

I know what you will say
I hear your voice
The words you choose
The way you say it
I know lover of loves but still . . .

I find myself without word
Without the right word
Collecting words
Flowing over as bath in play

There is *this* in me
I cannot say
The prodigal word
Said and loved
And loved it all

Still my lover of loves
Let me say that loving you
Has been the unwrapped gift
The inner mantle
The oblique lines that cross
Every loss that is also the living

When our forms have their due
The vespers scented candled hue

These things such things shot through
All I can do is inlay
My beating down heart in you

Second Sight

At times we have a second sight
We think we are the beginning
But rarely do we traverse
The wonderland of that exquisite pain

Here is the pricked needle
Into the fabric of you
Thread as fine parched hair
Pulled through
Weaving in and out of the destination
This comet of eternal dying

There are such beginnings
Unremarked
The first cracked egg
All tawny gilded yellow
Gelled encased sunset
Inside thin white hibiscus shell

Wrap your fingers around mine
Wrap your legs around mine
Wrap your tongue around mine
Nothing of me is closed

Rose Candoglia

If I could kiss you the rest of my life
A constant circulation of our skin
Small breaks for food
Artisan bread
Where the olive fats invade the air pockets
I would be happier than any happiness

You may say I am impractical
That there are other things to do
But why can't we work with constant kiss
As the gardener rakes over the stones
A fevered way
A pattern that works
Forever anew

The hummingbird kiss
The pebbled hiss
This this this
Your lip touch bliss
The stairs may vanish
But the bed is forever

Let's kiss and drink
And kiss all the more
Butterflying our lower backs
In the *this*

I could chase you into heaven
But let's not run
Too much work
Much too much fuss

Just the cusp
Of your quarter opened
Rose Candoglia marble
Only my lip can part
Then I would be happier than any happiness

I Am So in Love with You

It means . . .

To see your photos
To love them
To forget
To be reminded
To look for the first time
Every time
Your face
Captured motion
To love again

It means . . .

To hear your history
To know your stories
To absorb them
The lengths of your life
To forget
To be reminded
To hear for the first time
Every time
Each line of your life
To love again

It means . . .

To be within your time
To listen close
To recall the passages
The inflections of your voice
The when and where
The how
You tell your stories
I close my eyes
I know the sound of you
The drop and rise
The pause and pain
I *need* to remember them all
To forget
To remember again
I am so in love with you

The Traveler

At present
I am riding in a taxi
Long stretches of land
And all I can do is think of you

My tired collapsed happy body
Can sleep soon
And dream
Of our days before
You have taken its everything

In a little while
A long soak all heat
Thinking of the way you rest your head
The sound of drawn water
Steamed tiled artifice
Fingers trace the half-sensations
Fogged up mirrored condensation
No echoed infinity
Only the now

When I finally crawl under
Crisp sheets starched and white
I will think how
You pulled my offering
To the center of my collarbone

That dent of bone
At the center of my neck
Touched
Dangling silver necklace
Your inner rhythm sway
Sliding in and out

Love lengthening
Contracting
Lengthening soon
Of the memories fixed
In my figure's fatigue

Every facet feels your touch
Backs made of your magic
Waists living on your borderline

I hope to be home soon
And drag my fingers across
Your living plane
So that I can understand
The way the clay is pressed
To make the sculpture
Nothing is as smooth as it looks
Texture belies your power

All ridges and waves hardened into metal
All your fingerprints
All your pressure
All your touch
All of you
A lifetime ago
Poured into me

Paradise

I look at your face turned upside down in ecstasy
You unable to focus on anything
Except the intensity of your pleasure

The best vantage is between your unlatched legs
Continental drifting
Dividing
Forming
Oceans flowing
Puddles of thawed ice
The first world reformed through pleasure

With each hand
Compressed
Life-taking hold
I pull your foundation close
Tight against mine

My eyeline encompassing
Unfurling
Merging
Your waist to your face
The felt event horizon
Beyond perception
Time reformed through pleasure
And I lose myself too

Realize that the highest satisfaction is looking at your face
In ways most never do
In that closeness
Where passion, surrender
Are thrown wide
And the very soul of you rises

Afterwards
Let us come down to earth
Laying as we explore
Half awake
Steeped in sleep
Television flickering
Drinks and dying down holding
Hands roaming
Then reverie

We Know Who We Are

When you gave yourself to me in victory
The world within turned inside out
The last is the first and the first is the last

We know velveted damson
We know blood on the lips
We know iridescent heliotrope
We know winter's bay
We know breathing as sight
We know taste of nectar

When I gave myself to you in victory
The world within turned inside out
The last is the first and the first last

Where are you dear one?
Are you resting close by?

The Moon

Last night
Nearing sleep
I found myself walking through a cave
En-framed by wilting sunflowers
Deeper colors as they die
The yellows intensify

But I cannot help but drift into the moon
I only think of making love to you

At the other side
Alleys
Pathways
Sidewinding streets
Cafes
Poured drinks
Bodies in motion
The breeze chills and awakens
Lives
So many lives I will never know
Filled with inner plains of story
The courtship and the kingdom
Binding fate and brevity

But I cannot help but drift into the sea
I only think of you enchanting me

Everything is contrast and symmetry
Chaste reflections
The water droplet on knife's edge
Falls on terracotta
Laid before I was born
These things sink like stones
The organic unities
The unknowing acts
The underlying lullaby
So much unsaid
Permanence and change
Gifted navel oranges
Given yesterday
Perfect color
Soon they will intensify
All living and dying
Do and have done
Docile playful rounded fruit

But I cannot help but drift into the air
I only think of you at my heart everywhere

Sometime soon
Your body between mine
No distance
All time
Stretches of the enjoined kind
Cavernous laughter
The soaked-up edge of your inner thigh
Reaching the amen of you
Worlds of overgrown gardens
The banquet drink
All colors intensify

Before we come through the other side
Centuries I could bathe with you

Today among the Roman ruin
I thought again
The architect of your essence
Change and permanence
The landscapes and catacombs
Fresh mint dipped in oil
Crust of bread pressed olives
Shining blissful mouthing lips
Even this reminds me
The bone shot canopy
Embodied soliloquy
Textures embracing
Needful night

Tonight
I will sleep beneath the stars
Dreaming of your night and day afterglow
Thinking of lives I will never know

But I cannot help but drift into the moon
I only think of making love to you

The Un-Perishing

Ours is the un-perishing
Dropped dice
Shaking the gold
The percussion's densities
Ripped open exposed circuits
Bricks and mortar
Ours is change
Defeating change

You have always been
Every reflection of my face
The sight of you craved
The world entire swallowed
Bending constellation
You are place and orbit
Extending
I can and cannot survive
But that is the way of animation

My body could turn to dust
Feed the earth
Enter another sort of time
Become wildflower
And I would still be I
Retaining you
In the orbit

Your soul could melt in warming earth
Extinguished ice cap
Turned into roaring waves
Eroding the last continent
Biblical floods dry
You could become the trace in the sediment
Still you would be you
You would retain me
You are the remainder
Forever the touch of your lips
On the bones of my shoulders

Nothing undoes us
We are the undoing
We are the ends of the other
You begin in me
I end in you
You do your touch
I do the gaze that is all your own

Your face
Always your face
Ending my world

The Envy of Recollection

The rolling world of my soul
Has become material
Pulled down quicksand
The envy of recollection

Come close
Fold memory into infinite box
Become my every place
And this soul will be itself again

Come close
You are the lineament of the timepiece
The heavy blade
The robbed sentiment
The laid down dream

Come close
I wish you the jab and the break
You are iron ore melted
Removing my sentiment
Sign of my loss

You dip and dive
Sling and subdue
How can you catch me?
I never began

Never left
Never began

I cannot remember
The day you washed me from the silence
Lifted my body out of stone
I became the relief
The passing hour
Weeping the ancient matter

One day
Your spirit will taste of honey
Slowing past me
In thick gowned amber
You are
The envy of recollection

You Are . . .

You are reams of freshly printed paper
The arrangement on my desk
Bundled covers and hidden things
You are my hand collecting my hair
Exposed jawline

You are overgrown grass
Too green it pops
Slow Chartreuse growing between
The stone walkway

You are the blue stones
But only when wet
Shining new animal
Slithering across
The surface of the moon

You are foreign, uncharted
The unknown variable
The last page of every book
The first sip of every wine
Charging the palate
Preparing the night of laughter

You are the last exhibit in the last museum
The drama of sculpted death

Every moment of captured sinking
You are sex

You are the impenetrable thicket of wild mist
Falling upon the day
You are the final act of every play
Still you are opening night

You are fabric smooth, crushed, bundled
The warmth out of the dryer
You are the drawn bath
The first to enter the water
And it is perfect heat
Finally, the right heat
The right everything

You are the chill when the cream of fragrant lotion
First touches the breast
You are the power of verse
You are the ending sonnet and the sonnet's end

You are chrysanthemum, gardenia
Any scented spinning nirvana
You are galloping horses
Before the crack and the tame

You are the candy jar
All the lemon sweet sour candies
Shafts of delight
The scream
You are the first *eros*
The never before and the in-between

At Your Word

At your word
My lips became clove oil and sweet orange
Burning away in hidden fire
I taste to become the closest to you
Ecstasy and elegy

At your word
I became a ghost
Mortal presence forever perishing
Flying into your thicket
Without motion

Loving you
Is the enclosed tagine
Raided with fragrance
Reanimated as sky

When did you become the air emptied of gravity
Ginger and dark wine
The first of all time?

Paradise: The Shared Poems of Artist Carol Scott & Caitlin Smith Gilson

Stardust, **by Carol Scott**

Phantom Touch

In the steam of the shower came your phantom touch
I stayed until it was cold nearly drowning in ice
Even then I felt you in the shiver
Muscles contracting into slow moving glacier
What am I to do
Either hot or cold
Your trace apparition electrifies

The outnumbered are given more relief
Quick and bitter under the tongue . . .

It is you in every reincarnation
Of my exhalation
In all climates past fatigue

If I were at your shoulder's dip, then you would feel
My own long descending blushed pink elocution
Immortalizing touch

Under cover I awake from dreaming and thought it was you
Your foot touching mine
Hand on my shoulder compressed
The perfect spooning pair
Memory so vivid
The felt heaven of your breath
Your ghost is not you

Hot reverberating
Power tingling from toes to nose
I dare not move
Stay

The outnumbered are given more relief
Quick and bitter under the tongue . . .

Let's Break Bread

When you butter your bread
It gets soft, loses its crunch
Except at the edges

All that tangy cream
The slice can hardly contain
Add honey and salt
Puckered jam

It needs to be cut in half
Spread apart
Unable to take the weight
Practically liquid
Melted risen pockets
Squeezed, eaten
Finger food

When you give your piece over
All buttered bun
Almost cake pure sweet
A trail of steam
A trace wafting to the ceiling
It is the essence of the ghost
Made of pressure and heat
Risen dough

Your face says it all
Lost in revelry
Behind La Gioconda's smile
Abandoned for the moment
Building echoes
Your eyes beyond focus
Opening without sight
Smiling, sighing
I enjoy the joy of you

What you do to me
Sacred body
Broke open body
Oh . . .
How I love your body

In All My Passion

In all my passion
Tomorrow
On the rooftop again
Every note sung
Beyond reach
Descending the stories
To the bottom of the sea
To find a pearl
Iridescent green
The color of emerald
And bring it home

Rare treasured
Prized
Now mine
Made to defend
Your irritation
Enclosing the intruder
In concentric circles of my affection

Wisdom of nature
The only jewel made
By living creature
Witnessed
Possessed, crowning
Round gem bottom
In all the possibilities of my diving . . .

Like All Good Stories

Like all good stories . . .

What about your body
What about your hands
Your body take you places
Your hands make you things

My face waiting to smile at you

Days go by
Working
Playing

Months go by
Plowing
Harvesting

What end?
Worthy of innumerable tears
Deserving abundant happiness

What meaning?
Epically mundane
Expanding universe

What order?
Stars compelling wishes
God activated soul

I will tell you my secret
I open my mouth
But nothing comes out

I was made, remade, living again
Is this the origin?
The closing down?
The what and the when

Stories always end
But the best story never does
Hands make things
They sow and plough
Work the day
But souls make love forever

You are your happily ever after
You are the rule by which others are judged
You are a spinning top of wondrous colors
You are Einstein with better hair
You are Socrates without the trial
You are mermaids playing in the surf
You are the heart of Venus pierced
You are choirs singing carols
You are angels on Christmas day

Most perfectly you

Goodnight Love Maker

Goodnight love maker
Dream maker
The stars swirling in melting cup overflow

Tears of your face
Tears of time
The hour of joy is yet to come

Close me and open
Maker of dreams
Enamored sleep
Chambered you descending the stair

My caught heart
Rests one fathom below
Where you are
In gold of lower sea

Dream for me life taker
Love maker
Song of you sunk down dying in bliss

My prayers are made of night sky
Hidden in longing
Years of my face

Untouched you
The hour of joy is yet to come

Stars are made to dream
Shooting wishes
Resting on the moon
Struck by the sun
Casting shadow embankments
Banking desires
Bounding joy you came

First dawn of the day you wake
Cause of future hope
Co-create grace
Good morning love maker

Wonder What It Is Like to Be You?

Wonder what it is like to be you?
To feel what you feel
See through your eyes

You are more important
Than the wind that blows
More important
Than the plant that grows
More than wonder
The golden heart sun
One times one

Who are you?
Discovery promised
Quaking
Love enduring baby-making
Throbbing partner
Flowing

What is it like to be you?
To create what you create
All I know is that you have me
Dancing on the tops of clouds
Sum into sum
Lover of light and form
Beat the brass drum

Clean clear resonating sound
Controlled contour
Descending heaven's gate

You are the undulating swerve
The conjugated verb
Want and need
Pacing satiating
Overflowing corollary
Eaten sweetened sucked
Cut strawberry soaked in lemon
Dancing on the tip of my tongue

You are the ascending ankle
The talus and the tendon
The stretched body in time
Every word that pleads
Moans and breeds
Whispered panting dream of my dream

Who are you as you are?
Lions' hips
Running clutching
Roaring
Velveted mound
Reflexed fluttering
Jam sugared finger lace
Twisted white muslin
Every pleasure
The trace
The trace
Just the trace of you
Through the wilderness of me

You are perfect uncut pattern
Harmonic sum
The life
Floating down to earth
As rain from the clouds
Welcomed by the desert

III

Woman, Behold Your Son! Behold Your Mother!

The Mother of God committed to writing neither her thoughts nor her love for God and her son, nor her soul's suffering at the Crucifixion, because we could not have understood, for her love for God is stronger and more ardent than the love of the Seraphim and Cherubim, and all the host of angels and archangels marvel at her.

—St. Silouan, *Letters*

Beautiful, **by Carol Scott**

Of Love and God

There is something about you
I could say it is an invisible thread
Some form of netting
Far below any reach
Connecting me to you
But it is not that
It is other

Not for a moment
Do you leave my thoughts
What I mean is that you
Do not escape the underlying thought
The constant undying record
That must be me when all is said and done
The sound wave below sound
Where I live as a soul
Inhabiting the world beyond Eden
You are grafted to the best of me
As branch healed with another
But it is still more

Even as I work and play
And become distracted by life
Subterranean you are
Taking root somewhere
More than mind

More than essence
Even more than my heart

But what is more than the heart
Is it the teardrop
The swelled and fallen tear
More than word
A compact perfect tear
Consummate angelic spirit
Fastened into me

I could say you are in my blood
But I already have that
Are you the inner gilding
Of my veins and arteries
So that you move seamlessly with my pulse
Beating in time with me

Even if in all poetry
It is the Beautiful
That your being moves in concert
And mine with yours
It is yet something else
Its joy could only be exsanguinated
Cut away from itself
A whole body reduced to thorn
Calvary and the Cross

Possibly because we live
Somewhere between Elysium and exile
In and out of time
That this hidden anchor is all out of reach
And when it plunges into the waters
And breaches space

It draws me into a land I have never known
But I have always felt its trace
This trail of ecstatic wandering
Unknown seductive grace

I do not know what inhabits you
I think it fills you, this place
Before my first thought
I was made of it
This place

There is something about you
A somewhere to you
A place in you
That is more than every waking thought
So I keep thinking about you
What exactly I think about
It does not matter
It is that you live below my lips
All speech emptied into the love of you

My Love for You Is Constant

My love for you is constant
Another presence in the room
It wakes with me
Sleeps when I sleep
But forever watchful
Always learning the ways
To cherish you more

Sometimes it shocks
Unsealing my growth plates
Taking my back to sweetness
Newness

For there is innocence in pain
In knowing
In heartbreak
In desire
There are reservoirs inside the good

Loving you
Loving you from afar
The sun is not seen
But it is felt
You are felt

You Are Creator

You are Creator
It is your immaculate being
When you are away from light and color
I know you to be homesick
A sailor too long at sea

Come tomorrow
Make the majestic world again
Spoil me in beauty
I am coming home
To creation through you
Spoil me mediatrix sweet and sacred

Douse me in color
Set my eyes alight
I cannot know
I watch
But it is still
A too perfect creation

Laughter Is Good

Laughter is good
It is the only good at times
That we need
It floats to the surface
A ringed preservation
This laughter with you

I will remember these long nights
Forgive me for keeping you
But your laughter is good

I can feel the sand this night
Tonight our laughter
Is the great protector
It is the guardian of all angels
We are for now too good
Too happy
To be inside the earth

Last night I worried for you
And cold crept into my chest
I fall asleep to forget
Still in waking it was there

How good today to laugh with you
A parade of laughter

Marching band and after band lining up
Forgive me
I have taken much of your day
But your laughter is good

Legacy of Your Rosary

Crown of Roses your design
Decades of your consuming fire
Entwined plight of the Holy Night
Garland infinity legacy of life
Annunciation
Fruit of the Mystery
Your art of love
The birth of our Savior

No one can do what you have done

Diamond beads pressed from coal
Say the word, satisfy our soul
The waters of the Jordan
Flowing wine of Cana
Fruit of the Mystery
Your art of love
Your heart transfigurement

No one can do what you have done

Into the muscle of your finger touch
Dream of your heart weeping foot of the Cross
The anguish in the Garden
Honeysuckle scent of wilting flower
Lying lifeless world of loss

False gods and power
The scourging at the pillar

No one can do what you have done

Reworked glowing time bead of the divine
Your seamless cloak in beaming globe
Fruit of the Mystery
Fruit of love
The descent of the Dove
Crown of heaven
Forever above

No one can do what you have done

Your rose garden of knotted cord
This October month of the plunged sword
Angels engulfed in tongues of pearl
Inebriate blood crystalline white and pink
Olive seed from the Garden of Gethsemane
Pressed crucifix of my ghost
Shining mystery of your incarnate Rosary

No one can do what you have done

The One Who Shares My Heart Can Make Anything

Your life well lived is my happiness
Your love of God will be my todays
Between sleep and sky
I will love and pray for you

I cannot count the tomorrows
That the fates allow
But your presence seems to ride time
Your purpose brings me back to life
Impact
Brighter, truer, felt

Your realism
Your compassion
Incense through night and day
I believe you can make anything

Your fantastical insights
Your guarded sweetness
Spirit given as gift
I love that the one who shares my heart
Can make anything

You soothe in my sorrow
Your love of body
All bodies in love

Your ways move
You move my mind and my heart
You have all the next moves

You move my body
Because my heart is permanently moved
Your beauty could make anything
It already has

You are
Ever grounded and always free
Quite simply you amaze me

More Than Modern

More than modern
You are the veiled future
So far ahead of the game
Writing the rules
Designing the moves
You will endure
You are no one's fool

Score of demons cannot repent
The eternal light under a tent
Stony faces
Boned veined hands
Dying as we lay
Dying asleep dying awake
The religion of boredom
The cult of the mundane

Then there is the Good of you
Dream of the unseen
Dreaming image garden shatter the view
Bathe the world in the True
Immaculate Heart of you

There is no captured reflection
You make the pattern
Break the form

You are concert
Symphony and rest
Every part mystery and blessed

You are never at a loss
You heart is too Good
The very Good and the great
It overwhelms fate
Pierced heart I cannot wait
Perfectly timed ahead of all time
Mother of God

The Perfect Fit

When you dance
Skin of my skin
Flesh of my flesh
At the sight of you
I forget to breathe
Anatomizing need
Only say the Word
Whatever you want I need

Warmed vibrating cacophony
Of your inner deed
At the sound of you
I forget to breathe
Broke open plead
The clutched embrace
Only say the Word
Whatever you want I need

Rosebuds basking in your sun
Fragrant transparency
Reed of your back
Dipping hip broken tree
At the touch of you
I forget to breathe
Only say the Word
Whatever you want I need

More than thought
More than sense
More than any *to be*
The perfect fit
You are anatomy

The Friendship in Christ

Dearest friend of mine
The moving image moves on
And I am woven into the soft
The deeper memory
The unearthed first death
The only one to survive

There will be decades that pass
Life has its lonely passage
Its corridors haunt without end
Ending in no room and no place
But I am living within the sanctity
Of your heart grieving its flowers
Into mine grieving time

There is no time here but expression
The texture of your living descending
As fingers dipped in oils of the Cross
Made with the body
Dwelt in the spotless soul
Anointing me in the beauty
Of your life

Loving you
Knowing the timeless heart
That lives inside

Your time-bound smile
I could fade into the forgotten
And remain the one made of sand
Stretched across the seas

Your words
Any of them
All of them
Have a way of landing in me
As long-traveled albatross
Flighted over oceans
To find ground

I rest in the thought of this
The image of that flight
A silent muscled contraction
Extending shadows
Over motionless stretches of sea

I could cry
Thinking of you and this
This image of you
Soaked smile of mind and memory
The sponged wine fell into my lips between stone and sky
I hold onto you as waters unmoved

The Foundress

Exquisitely unarmed in the estuary of the eternal
She said:
      I am within this life of yours
          Yours curled and carved and convened a sunlit heat within mine
          To shine
          To shine
          To shine into the depths of earth and bone
          Colder than winter's snow

The many chambered silence of heart and womb
Foreclosed our ancient tomb
The designated passenger
The bearer of all time
Redressed our guilt with unfinished gentleness
Lain on grass

In the dying
Titans heave the imperishable and are forcibly pulled in two
Essence thrown aside
Flesh collapsing like worn clothes kicked to the floor
We know nothing of what it means to surrender the ghost

Irremediably unprepared for what has shattered within each of us
And unstudied in the unrelenting gentleness
Pressing itself into our remaining shape and time
Whittling itself down along the line

Lowered through the veil of every generation
Pressed and dried hillside flowers
Pushed aside books and shuffled photographs forfeiting all recollection
Hushed into the many chambered corners of failure and love
His body and blood
In her body and blood
In our body and blood
Transmuting the grave
Redeem us in our unreadiness
Our Lord of the Lost and Found

My Child, My Little One: *Ad Jesum per Mariam*
for U.M.

Long ago I was young
I did not know it then
But it was for you
To be this dying comet of love
Finishing my soul in you

I was created for you
Before you were born
Made by love for you
Created by you
This is how time works

What ends always begins again
The hours we have now
Have always been the only play
The only stage
The only way home

These hours together are my dying
These hours my conceiving
The curve of your cheek
Every nectar-scented kiss
Your unmistakable face
I would know you in blindness
In the night of my mind

In you I have lived
Loved even more

I was born that day
Your touch encased me
Enclosed me in your littleness
You have been a rose
The bud of a rose
The remaining scent after the waterfall

And still you encase me now
That half of me halved again
That day

This my child, my little one
Is how time works
We are measured in giving
Time with you is my only dying
Loving you has been the only form of love
That is too good
To land anywhere on earth

Because of you
Even in the grave
I will float into sky and to river
Live my cherished one by water

So that I may come to you always

The Axe and Tear

There is something to the sound of metal hitting the air
Released from its coverall
I can hear it now

I feel the end nearing but I am washed in love
This is the end bearing down but I could not love you more
Every teardrop oceanic tides drowning infinite gods

This sense of you
The held relief of you
Is made on another ground
It wraps its arms and becomes All Soul

But there is something lurking in the air
Cold around my features pressed belly of the beast
Of tales long ago and older demons hollowed and alive

If only your eyes could take me and remove the end
The slide of metal and neck
Young deer safe in the hide

What is it about sensation and selection?
The solidified drawn curtain
The shifting seats
The spectators and the spectral
Under the axe of one centurion

What is it about knowing without power?
The senses never marred with age and never graceless remains
I could not love you more than at that moment when . . .
But my head is nowhere to be found

Some weight I cannot know has laid on my chest
An instrument of time
Reminded fabrics rough yet smooth

In April love was born and love died
In April I confide my heart now everywhere
In the sheets
In the baking scents
In the way your kiss comes on steep
Stronger than the cathedral bell
Ringing through me in rainfall sweet

I cry for you my love
Cry because time cannot remain our friend
If only my tears were graces and they could fly
As angel in the night

If only my tears were a single grace
They are only the water and the salt
Now animating my body
My tears must be my soul
For I cannot take another April
When love was born and love died

I cry for you my love
I am made of tears cascading for you
Tasting of the time of your lips
When the sense of you worked into me another ground
Rolling hill and vale and you became All Soul

But soon the angel will be gone
For we cannot live on weeping

Behold: The Shared Poems of Artist Carol Scott & Caitlin Smith Gilson

City Park with the Grandsons, **by Carol Scott**

The Night of Blessings

Good night
A simple phrase
More than passing melody
It is vigil, protection
A blessing over you

Wishing you good night
As your mind retreats
As all of you becomes
The dark north wood
The unknowing shrine
The offerings of your life

The good night dresses the luminous
It is the odyssey of the holy
Beneath every fable and lullaby
It comes upon as warmth
And wraps the particular
Shrouded graces
Easing into you
The great silence

Virgil went down into the deep
Dante blocked by an unholy three
The emptied way
The place of no return

We may plummet into this sleep
Where the carnal growls
And tug us into death
The terrors of willful night
The evils of the day

But tonight is the nocturne
The forever gentle
Good night means I pray
With everything I am
To transfer the being inside me
To come to you
To inhabit your vulnerability
To give you the elixir of our love
The inner sanctuary of my waking
Watching over you

Good morning gives you hope for a new day
An invocation for all goodness and light
Calling forth adventure
Prometheus unbound
Beginning play
Fresh and rested
The stone has been rolled away
Seized in glory
I will see you

I see you and say
Loved both night and day
I acknowledge your being
The tone of your voice
Wonders of you
Your face answers
How many hellos?

How many goodbyes?
I sigh if it is you

You Are All Beauty to Me

You are all beauty
The wax releases its scent with heat
All the countries exploration
Nothing matches you

I have taken my candlelight
Into the geography of the soul
Miles into the earth
Wrapped around caverns
Into the sight defeating all vision

I have my held breath at the low door
The topography of the sung word
The repetition
The risen voice
The release into chord

You could not be more beautiful
But the earth
Is the only home I have ever known

Your song is from the angels
I hear church bells
They sound like your heart
Beating strong, loud
Calling me

The spirit of you comes to me
I see your colors as prisms of the universe
Light as pretty as sunrise
Wilding passion released
Eloquent, smart, some would say the vision
Body, mind, and meridian
Infused to perfection

The Vision Flowing Gold

There are bands of gold around your fingers
Flowing torrent
Draped body
An invitation
Treasure lit

You shine as if all the tears hidden in the seas
Beyond human capacity
Have merged and become
The place between nature and grace
As the sun is to God

When I am with you take the gold from your shoulders
Place it on my waist
Flows of time and change
Divine muses telling stories

Then I will see again
Hear again
Understand fragrance
How it cradles us
Wrapping itself in redolence
I will taste
Touching fields and waters
The fruit of our labors
And sleep

The long sleep
Given to the universe

When stars collide
Lovers become the merged eye of heaven
Or they collapse and die
Your gold survives
Honeycomb to the bee
Your feet in wells of ink
Dipped in precious metal
Forging the future

Past childhood memories become gold
My father would take me
To the stone grotto on Rampart Street
Wet rocks held
What seem to be
Hundreds of candles
Flaming prayers
Lit by the faithful
Flaming visions of the Holy Spirit
I wonder if heaven smells like melting candlewax

Everywhere Else

Everywhere is restlessness
Swollen and drawn in faces
The edge of the earth
Brutal and rushed packed cattle

Everywhere is frailty
Undefined blocks of grey
Suffocated sold world
Smoldering in the last fire

Everywhere is disease
Soulless slotted word
Metal prongs
Piercing the masses
Heaving the last sparks

I need to find my way home
The longest day
Legs buckled underneath
If only you were next to me
I would have the strength
To curve my body around yours

I need to find my way home
Sadness encamped the night
Terrible fright

But I can crawl
Just the thought of you

I need to find my way home
My sleeping and my waking
My compassion
I could run days
Just the image of you

The thing about happiness
All of it contains a locket of sadness
Buried away from the beginning
Such is life
We do not find it until later
After the rains
If we are lucky
It may become a treasure

You are my happiness
My treasure
The locket between us
Is made of pure gold
There is no way to mine for it
It is the mystery of our love

I am always with you
Watching your back
The little kiss
Tingle on your neck or whisper in your ear
A kind smile from a stranger

Serendipity
a smell, a song, an unspoken thought
I am your home

Fate

I feel in you
The everything of universe and dance
Fated fatal loving glance
An inner knowing
Beyond image and imagining
Glowing, flowering

Running would have been useless
Our legs took us in a circle
Ending in you
I cannot envision the action
The sequences and layers
That made you happen

The stirred one-word unfathomed chance
And you, the gift of you

Always now
Found without being lost
Probability infinitely doubtful
If my step were too quick
If I had not prayed
If it had or had not rained
If the sun were too high
If we had not said
The requisite hello or goodbye

The stirred one-word unfathomed chance
And you, the gift of you

Prayer sweetly answered as God plays his game
Beauty magnifies beauty
Love graces love
Immeasurable mystery
Too many moves to plot
Beyond the stroke of thought
Fated fatal loving lance
All that is needed
All I can do
Is enter the gift of you

The stirred one-word unfathomed chance
And you, the gift of you

The Bond of Unknowing

How do you experience what I know?
Be me
When I say
"Warm, bright, intense yellow"

My mind is a wondrous place
Floating, flying, flitting
Colors dancing and dying
Igniting the sun

Do you see the golden pigment on my canvas?
Gifting the described experience to another
Or looking at the same glow do you see what I see?
This bond of unknowing

Some things break the spirit
This reality below word
Is there more beauty than the actual image?
Always more than the actual encounter?
Is music better than sound?
Dancing better than walking?

Questions without answers and questions again

Your motion is my reason
Your energy is answered prayer

My heart is your breaking
Your life is prayer in motion
The beauty through and through
The actual encounter
The answer has always been you

My heart is your weeping
Your questions are the answer
Your giving is the gift
Your motion is the Cross
Your life is the prayer
My heart is your being
My long silence longing for you
This is my keeping

Questions without answers and questions again

The Morning Feel of Child You

The morning feel
Half-grazed touch across sunlit fields
It could shatter the earth without a sound
When you were born

Time is stretched by love and pain
Bribe me with your beauty
Resurrected lakes of lean blue
Lunging toned muscled wake
Shaking off the passing scene

I can throw you a lifeline
Dull the blade
Unfix time
Become prayer
Sign of the Cross
Cover you with kisses like Brancusi
Outwit the sin and the loss
Picasso's weeping woman
Never want you to suffer

I knew a boy who wanted to be God
All the time I had
This moment's rest
This past behind the past
In the universe of chance

Long ago there were fireflies
Floating above
Lengths of midnight hair woven into the canopy
The beginning and end of me
When you were conceived

IV

My God, My God, Why Have You Forsaken Me?

I, too, stood on the sacred image. For a moment this foot was on his face. It was on the face of the man who has been ever in my thoughts, on the face that was before me on the mountains, in my wanderings, in prison, on the best and most beautiful face that any man can ever know, on the face of him whom I have always longed to love. Even now that face is looking at me with eyes of pity from the plaque rubbed flat by many feet. "Trample!" said those compassionate eyes. "Trample! Your foot suffers in pain; it must suffer like all the feet that have stepped on this plaque. But that pain alone is enough. I understand your pain and your suffering. It is for that reason that I am here." "Lord, I resented your silence." "I was not silent. I suffered beside you."

—Shūsaku Endō, *The Silence*

Chalices Burning, **by Carol Scott**

Last Evening Shelled the Sun

Last evening shelled the sun
Cracked open skeleton
Felled ambushed tears
Burning fuselage
Downed
When I went to pray

My heart touched my knee
Blood of me
Sorrowful
Raining organ
In the last plead

This is not a letting go
It is a sinking
Low lonely blinking
Dreamless standing down

All of this has me
Weightless
Floating into ice rings
Concretized dying
Moving the furnishings

Today
If only your skin

Under the shadowland
Your Halcyon
Liquid confession

If only your spices
Scenting the pan
Your voice
Litany of the skies

If only your whirlpool
Vanquishing the ghost
Your legs
Dissolving the powder keg

If only you
Shipwrecked bliss
And you

I am in the carved-out endgame
Losing my life
The sun broke in two
This life I knew

There is a land for the living
And a land for the dead
Tread lightly
I am halved in two
If only
I could make love to you

For the Time Being

For the time being
Every bend of my body will howl
As wolves to the moon

How do you expect me to sleep
When my skin rebels
When it betrays
Needing your fingered press
More than mine
More than the soul which keeps it

My hands and walk
They abandon their animation
Peeled off layers of order and reason
The keeper of the keys
The seat of wisdom
Unreasonable demanding want
Skin of my soul
Howl me into shade
Howling for you

I cannot row the ocean
Glide the thousand leagues
Survive the iced waves
Crests and perilous falls
The animals of the deep

Material jaw violet blood gnashed teeth
Jonah swallowed in the belly of the beast

I cannot yet fly
Ascending bartering cry
My verb constricted
Not a word more
Not even a sigh
Begging body
Bruised by sound
Even the bed and the covers hide
Howling to the chorus on the mountainside

My Father

Tunneling to the end
If I lift my head
What remains slams to the floor
Made of the matter of *this* and *this*
Dead two years
Hands on my face, on yours my palms
Stretched fingering disbelief
Nails as cleaned stone
Your cheekbones rough as they were
And all our tears cannot unlearn
The path of descent

You have been pulled out from beneath
Too much of the uprooted ground
For the earth to tilt back
It cannot save
Powerless you come
A gaze without sight
Every look replete with agony
Made of the matter and the mind
Devoured in the infinite wreath
Of things to come

Can we not collide?
Stash our souls into the other
And survive the last temptation

Love cannot be *this* and *this*
For you are shadowing you
Peeled film cascading
The coverall of weeping child

Can we not collide?
Made of might and star
Your eyes the resigning feature
The doorway subsiding
Christ in far off land
And my sorrow trawls the deep

We are made of the weak
Each heart weaker than the next
Their power is to release us from power
To revive the soul as it convenes the body
Empty the wounds of our hands
Of our sides
Selves made of shivering grain flung from power
Into the earth purged of gravity
Into the void that ends inside
The Christ in far off land

Your terrible sorrow comes upon me as fog
Towed out into the middle of your soul
And left to weep the carnival
Twisting undressed socket
Electrical pulse
Bodies made of *this* and *this*
Dying inside the dying sun

If only we could live and be
And forward the earth into permanent futurity
Skin of geometric dimensions

Folding into sweetest candy
To catch wisdom with painted sugar
Felled from sky
Rain in rundown suns
Thousands of suns
Stepping into thistledown clouds

One day we will jump to the top
To the terracotta tiles that cover the church roof
Lighter than air and sliding down
Becoming a slope of snow in the Alps

My Lord you pulled the rug out from beneath me
Oh, we collide until we dry into ash
Undo the die that has been cast
This weakest love weakening
And all our tears cannot unlearn
The path of descent

The Weather Has Finally Shifted

The weather has finally shifted
I woke to the winds' desecration
Creating whistles, guttural shrieks
Through the slats

Many spaces can it breach
In the doors and in the windows
An invading invisible army of sound and ice

I will be a fool today and jump into the waves
Dip my head until my ears become numb
Until I lose sight of what it means to concentrate
Consummate gulf of being
Forsaken but holy

It is far too cold today
Too much life has run away
But I love the sun
Make love to me

I have no idea how to be warm again
I am a fool in covers thread bare
My lips are chapped scanning a room of things without you
Time is the forsaken passion
Make love to me

The Winter's Chill

In the winter's chill
The atrium of my heart
Has no summer birds
All flew south for winter
Back to you

Somewhere in one of those dusky afternoons
As round and smooth as robin's egg blue
You replaced my bloodstream
The way I heat my body
With longing for you

What a cunning trick
You are the aspect of the circle
The sextile of Jupiter
You stole June and July
And took all my warmth

I need more than the spiced balm
Conjured vision of you
I am clothed but naked
Bundled but bare
Rivulets of ice
Coating the stair

If I could hibernate

A polar bear fast asleep
Waiting for your body
To thaw me into spring
If only I knew how to wait for you

If I were numb, I would be the cold
The emptied missing opacity
Your thumbscrew curve
Winged turn with forefinger burn

The faucet drips
It could freeze tonight
Your absence is twice frozen ice
Madness, teeth chattering
Cadmus sewing the dragon's teeth
This ceiling all ceilings must burn
Long curls of finely separated wood
An effigy in flame and allegory

If I survive the winter solstice
Then you can be mine
Burning scent of pine
The tempo of your hips
You can lead, move your body
All your heat, the hotseat
Furnace of my greed
Wild, combustible
Flammable, electrical fire
I am thieving all your heat

Today I Was Late

Today I was late
A poor soul
Lost in the depths
Young man not thirty
Jumped on the track
What else but oblivion

There is no sweetness
He waded into the shallows
And sunk
No water to float
What else but fallen

How did he decide
The moment before
The hour
The day
Always the day
If only there was a way
To lure back time
Wade back
Back in line
Back to home and to life

His mother out of place
Somewhere in the inner space

The outer spaces
The heart cannot break
It simply implodes
Sunken stone
The earth's loneliest passage
Only heaven knows

Was there nothing left
No creation to tread
No laughter
No broken bread
Nothing to stave off death

Did he know love
The close under closeness
The candlelight
Moonlight
All lights
Did he know comfort
A home to himself

The inhaled scented bed
Clean and fresh
The dizzy hint of new day
Was there no lover
No peace
No child
No half glanced bliss

Unknown life
Once in a lifetime life
Never again life
Mangled bruised broken life
The house of eternal life

Ripped from its sockets life
The marrow below life

This life
Forgive us God
Forgotten now for we are late
It is getting late
The train and bus and trains again
All to circumnavigate the death on the track

What if I were motionless in the middle of steel
Half a body
Departed soul
Blood on the tracks
Vortex of lack
Slack jaw nothing
What if I were the dying?

If only I could lure back time
Half a line
Who can pay the heavy fine

The heart caves in
Yelping bellowing grief
It cannot lick its wounds
Too entrenched
Bleeding furiously
Mounting chasms
The blood loss
The lost son
Once an infant
Small as two hands
Promises sunk as stone
Too far to catch again

God there needs to be a God
To atone for this loss
Dropped stone
Wishing well of sin

God there needs to be a God
Bring this son home
Forgive us God
This life
Forgotten now
It is getting late

I Could Have Perished in My Sorrow

I could have perished in my sorrow
The day you died
Collapsed body
Undernourished
Broken at the window pane

Blood of my blood
I bleed for you
Weep for you
Offer my stripped down
Ripped out joints for you
If only I could
Seep into deep earth
Where you are
Dust of my dust

I think we lay in the center of stone
Sleeping without dreaming
Deep into cold

Everything in my crushed wailing organ
Cannot be touched
Too cold and too hot
Too near and too far
Ephemeral and weighted anchor
I cannot begin to breathe

Snowfall cannot survive the sun
Melted water
Feeding the soil
Depleted devastated sucked down soul
Drained into weeds

I could have withered in my sadness
Returned to the earth
I would
If deals could be made
If life worked in that kind of trade

No one should outlive the little ones
The holiest of human beings
The child made of substance and dream
She can run along the sunlit hills for hours
Leaping and free

Corruptive life
A thief in the night
Completing the fall
Gall on my lips
That day of all days

Tonight I lay with you in the center of stone
Sleeping without dreaming
Deep into cold

Apocalypse

When next I see you do take care
Only a glimpse of fire in your reflection
An incanted slanted writhing back
Snatched confection
And I . . .
The lost and the lack

The die has been cast

The fated conjured sight of you
The unmatched liquored scented brew
Dancing bodied incantation
And I . . .
The lie and the imitation

The die has been cast

Fingers fixed in motion
Sorceries sipped and hexed
Flesh in the push down
And I . . .
The bruised and the ground

The die has been cast

The tongue mapped inner cry
The singing ringing jut of bone
Hip flask inebriate sigh
And I . . .
The whip and the sky

The die has been cast

Sap of the twilight god
Tumbling tower of haste
The Rubicon of spoken shadow
And I . . .
The want and the waste

The die has been cast

All earth's firelight collects around your face
The loss
The loss
The loss of grace
The mortal spell
The pinprick no return
Dipped in honey and gall
Tossed into the wishing well
And I . . .
The failed and the fall

Alea iacta est

Time

Time slipping through fingers
Falling from eyes
It knows no master
Time
Time
Time is the bed of sighs

Forsaken

The God of melted snow has infinite tears
Every spring when the first leaves christen the trees
Our Lord weeps the nectar of Being

If you let me become
The grace of the moon
Resolving into you
Drifting leaves
Easing my compassion . . .

If you let me become
The warmth of your indigo
Condensed rings of slumber . . .

If you let me become
The once was
Covering you
Covering me . . .

Then I may know the springs
Before the Crucifixion

Before the saw-dusted cleaved artery
Spilt its unspoken Word
Beneath the elegy of your leaving
Blood of our making

Uncollected heavy end
Muted in silent fall

My lover is bruised fragrant mind
Terminals of time

My lover is the time that you died
The time of you

My lover is the soil of this earth
The remaining wintered vigil

My lover is emptied form
And poured vessel

When the color-pressed clay
Burned and fired itself into the end
My lover was endless waking
The keeping and the closing
The wilderness of you

I am the Sorrow of Homecoming

I am the sorrow of homecoming
The force of life
Gravity
The one unavoidable scene keeping the earth

This power is indifference or malevolence
One of them
None of them
For thine is the kingdom

Now is the time to be plowed into the mud
This force uprooting the earth
Into blocks of unyielding ground
Pulling and heaving my shins
Through overgrown tombs
Till they bleed the hint of the bone
The glint at the knob of my knee
Till it shows its isolating bridal white irony

I was away far away on the terrace of the moon and bells
Spells and spells and spells
Of sleeping, waking, un-forsaken
Far far away in the land after ends

But I am coming home to the sorrow of things
Heading to their ends

To their ends
Eloi, Eloi, lama sabachthani

If only I had cloaked my legs in clay hardened and fired
If only the stove burned pitch black
If only I had shoved my feet, my legs, my shins up to my knee
Then as I trod this earth siphoning down and down
Down the gravitational pool
I would not glance the corpses of the past
Catching up in threes
Pulling me into them on this the longest way home

Ruiner of Prayer

What is it that I want?
Is it that I must have you God
That I desire you long buried long ago
That the matter is closed and settled
Then I can dream and hit the ceiling

This waiting is focused mist
This promise is pain
Let the matter be closed
Let it shut down
So that dreams are swift and short
The babe with broken neck and no feet

If I knew that you had left the room
Long ago years before I was born
So that ancient is the matter of my heart
And the columns that shore the temple
Crumble and no longer hold
That the matter is closed
The Word was said but no longer heard
The fairytale of the holdover
The lost word before waking

I need the matter closed
Because if you die

I will die in the matter and the life
And sleep the sleep of rest without dream

The elegy of the closed case
Breaking into me as I breathe
I will never see it through
Push it down below my feet
I can put the pages down
And ahead of me is water
Burial of the deep

Why can't the matter be closed?
Sealed unattended book of life
Pushed aside
One dusty shelf of insignificance
The memory after the fact
None of the dance
Why must I keep you with me
This one act of the will
Threaded between two seas
Between words and deeds
Of the God who does nothing
And everything
Depending on the way I bleed

You who lay mute
All voice and all silence
You the unending rotating spiral
Drilled down into the base
Ruiner of prayer

Forsaken: The Shared Poems of Artist Carol Scott & Caitlin Smith Gilson

The Vespers, by Carol Scott

I Am a Mortal Being

I am a mortal being watching death
You deny and plead
Seen over and under
The truth replaced with the comfortable lie
Life incised
One butterfly cabinet of pins and wings

Are you the one to die or mourning left behind?
Crucified in your sleep
Crouching hind quarters
Ending the same
Do not go
We were once immortal
This past before all past

Bodies thrice dying
Destination long gone
Lasting silence
Lips laced
The Word ahead
And the dead under the dead

Sorry for your loss
Cannot reflect the cost
My other was not misplaced
Everything born moves to its loss

Do not go
Who can bear the cut down flowers
The fields of fallen hours
Can't we dive into our Eden and you always be mine?

If you stay, we can be waterfall
If you stay, every star ancient at the manger
Will shine on friend and stranger
If you stay, death cannot part us
Can't we dive into Eden tonight and breathe our new sight?

We will dive into Eden and always be life
Wish on that star lover
Wish on it for me
Death cannot part us
Dive into that star tonight and everything is music

What Is It?

What is it?
Has your soul gone out the window
Transmuted the glass
Is it flame on the iron cross bar
Your animation fleeing closer to mercury than the moon
Dark of the day of my body
Who are you when the sun comes pouring in?

What is it?
Have you become the future living in the past
What wound up ribbon of tales raids your mind
Divested love, registers of love
Degrees and ranges of being in time
Light of the night of my mind
Who are you when the sun comes pouring in?

What is it?
What knotted wood is braille to your fingers
Where were you when the tidal wave came
When the floor made sky
Air of the silence of my angel of death
The groundless gaping river of forgetting
Who are you when the sun comes pouring in?

What is it?
I am left in the dark palming the walls

Are you the fruit of the tree?
Taste of the feast of my passion?
The rain shaped arches pelting the ground?
The sting of a thousand resin-stained honeybees?
Who are you when the sun comes pouring in?

What is it?
What imageless longing lays out your thoughts?
Letters of the words of your book
What somber dream rings the refrain?
Where is your shelter and your heart?
Hollowed tunnels of passing trains
Ferried passengers after life afterlife
In everything there are remnants of shade
Passion holding you here
What spirit below the floorboards calls you?
Who are you when the sun comes pouring in?

Tears Have Drowned My Soul

Tears have drowned my soul
None will win
Death knows both sides

New Saint Joan
Rosaries on rosaries
Pleading intreating buried knees

History of hate
Kill ten
Kill a hundred
Kill a thousand
How will it end?

Lord have mercy
How can we ask?
When we give with one hand
And take with the other

Blood on our hands
Blood of the Holy Lands
Evil in our teeth
Evil in our minds
Blood spilling
Chilling our souls
Cursing our bones

Piles of bodies
Burned as trash
How can we last
Lives reduced
The wisp of an eyelash
Terrorizing flash of metal
Death ever unsettled
Motherless earth of ash
Burning rains
Recollected transport trains

Wicked raid of mind and soul
Goodness, Truth, and Beauty sold
Have mercy on us

Alpha and Omega

Blowing wind and unseen power
Felt force lifting and carrying flight to oblivion
My beginning and my end
Why have you forsaken me?

Evening light of paper planes
Shot through the air
Simple heart
Recollections of blue sky and day bright

Stilled night into unseen weakness
Felt surrender descending into temporality
Metallic fuselage hurling through clouds

Complex heavy soul
White of the earth
Night without light
Coolest muted fabricated and powerless

Every experience has its opposite
Every sensation another pole
You have been my up and my down
My living and my dying
My beginning and my end
Why have you forsaken me?

Be Aware

Folly and fools
A zoo of deadly charm
Poverty of the intellect
In the age of consent

The gaps expanding burnt up energy
Moral despair pull up a chair
Hanging life fallen down
The mimic's frown

When my ship collided
The heaving wood impaled itself
Mouthed in flame

Naïve hope
The rifle's polished scope
The guillotined sleepwalker
When suffering is the same

Blinded pathos
Unoccupied ambiguous need
Scattered seeds of time
When now is nevermore

Be aware
The revolving door

Is the circus fair
Death comes with your stare

Unforsaken

I am waiting for you to take me as you did
As it was before I lost my kind
I cannot wake the broken order
Corded thread of my ache
Let me ride again your curve
To become what we were
The morning before the end
If only the concave kiss
Here-and-there flesh
Clever pressed
Returned its crush of love

What *was* lover
Is buried beneath the earth
Heated on coils of fire
Shadows in satin mesh
Sadness unto death

What *was* lover
Is every spiraling gulf
The ship of me in pleading wish
The unattended sensation
The last Cross
The lost station
I am still waiting
All licked crystal white without a container

Spices packed in straw
Buried beneath the earth

Things have a way of dying
Running their course
Falling apart
I pull the pieces of you near
I pull you together
You
I pull you close
And you pull me apart

Can't we be something else?
Even if the moon loses it light
You are more than moon
More than earth

Tears wet my cheeks in sadness
Resuscitate me
I cannot breathe
You bring life to the dead
Have compassion on me

Most perfect soul
You taught the foolish that caused you pain
All perfected pleasures given again and again

I am waiting to take you as you are
Receive my love
Accept my kisses
I will take you as I did
I am not finished

V

I Thirst

Esther did not like love, she did not want to be in love, she refused this feeling of exclusivity, of dependence, and her whole generation refused it with her. I was wandering among them like some kind of prehistoric monster with my romantic silliness, my attachments, my chains. For Esther, as for all the young girls of her generation, sexuality was just a pleasant pastime, driven by seduction and eroticism, which implied no particular sentimental commitment. . . . The centuries-old male project, perfectly expressed nowadays by pornographic films, that consisted of ridding sexuality of any emotional connection in order to bring it back into the realm of pure entertainment had finally, in this generation, been accomplished. What I was feeling, these young people could not feel, nor even exactly understand, and if they had been able to feel something like it, it would have made them uncomfortable, as if it were ridiculous and a little shameful, like stigmata in ancient times. They had succeeded, after decades of conditioning and effort, they had finally succeeded in tearing from their hearts one of the oldest human feelings, and now it was done . . . they had reached their goal: at no moment in their lives would they ever know love. They were free.

—Michel Houellebecq, *The Possibility of an Island*

Crystal and Tabasco, by Carol Scott

All I Need

All I need is the thinking about your pleasure
The distilled spirit of your salts
Divesting time of its anchor
Drifting into the swirl at the center of the eye

Your peak is undiluted water splashed on my face
Cleansing the day
The story of weakened knees
A two-person play

A peerless engagement
Glossed silver tray, oriental bow
Stained glass, beveled edges
Lingering borderless touch
You become the lowered needle
Thunderstorm sound of vinyl

I am all things for you
Shaved white chocolate
Oxygenated fire
Blue base of the flame
Melting as I call your name

Madagascar

"For we are the aroma of Christ to God among those who are being saved and among those who are perishing, to one a fragrance from death to death, to the other a fragrance from life to life."

Cracked vanilla pod
Spread apart
Non-dominant hand holding the top down
Tensed reflexes
Flipping the jackknife to the smooth side
Contorted mirror catching your chin

Only sensation crawls to the boundary line

Blade down
Running it from the curled bottom
To the reliquary tip
River mouth of luscious relief
Dipping lip, vanishing point
White orchid piqued shrapnel
Bourbon tongued sleep
The smell of you
Beneath these upside-down trees of life

Only sensation crawls to the boundary line

Mystical Body of Christ

You are the vestment of my flesh
The secret vault of spirit
Praising the skin
Transfiguring mind into sight
Anima mea

You have moved through me as refreshment
Siphoning nectar hummingbird
Layer cake dripped ganache
An unpinned sash floating above the ground
Anima mea

You chaff my skin into spun silk
Thrust my soul twice into its body
Bone white wafer dissolving under the flesh
Anime mea

Without taste I am the three shades
Without you, flightless despair
Caught within the fowler's snare
If you wake I would sculpt you from memory
All cavern of sugared longing
Thrust upon my face
Anima mea

When you bring me back to being
I see you in the ancient satellite
As you should be seen
Halo of myth redeemed
Steeple bell in lonely windswept hill
Warmth of the fire
Mystical Body
Body of Christ
Anima mea

In the Days

"Take, Lord, and receive all my liberty, my memory, my understanding, and all my will—all that I have and possess. You, Lord, have given all that to me. I now give it back to you, Oh Lord. All of it is yours. Dispose of it according to your will. Give me your love and your grace, for that is enough for me."—Adrienne Von Speyr

In the days without us
Motion has become
Inset layers of wood engravings
One fit firm against the other

Of days inflicting days

Topics of hunger subdivided into priority
Avenues and attributes of desire
Strung along minutes confusing eternity

Of time endangering time

In the days without us
Winding circuit and grid
All the city lights go dark
Arch of being and hiking stakes

Of now dethroning now

Can't we become leaves of granulated sugar
Dissolving on lips
A spinning dervish
Making rings around my breast and hips

Of roofs under roofs

When it is the time of us
Be the oars gliding to the center
To the sound and to the pale
Carved painted sculls
Displacing these waters

Of gaps between gaps

Diving from the Ledge

I sit at the side of our bed
You gather the tufted corners unclothed
From one end to the other you move
You are the end of its magic
The mantic prayer

Your glass
Clear tinted artifact
The water of your lips and drink
I wait as crushed apple seed
Planted in the earth to sink

The hint of my being opened
Kissing the spheres that mark
Your upper and lower lives
Subterranean you are the air
The supplicant and the asking prayer

Propelled by you
Into the grain of my hands
The water from the glass
It cannot remain
Forever you circling the edge
All human all angel all animal
Diving from the ledge

Confession at Sea

Put out into the deep and let down your nets

You are the raked bow
Breaking the plane of resistance
Spools of vibrating off-white cotton
The vows of the earth towed behind you

Your intinction
Bread dipped in wine
Is the first sight of land from sea
After burial leagues deep
Moonraker sail
Hope of heaven

You are the bowsprit anchor
Descending beyond the vessel
Anointing my body
Blessing my soul
Sursum corda
Spice of the flesh
Click of tongue swish
Touching the flame
When I lick the sun
Breathe for me and bless my name

Trade winds circulate the coming winter's air
Let us make our way to Tenerife
To the painted market stalls and harvest fair
Your unbroken legs stretch forth our offering
Autumn of Christo de la Laguna
Yellow canary in winding tomb
Lost at sea
The older elegy
Your skin's confession
Haunting ship at evening speed

Deferred Gratitude: A Cycle

I. In the Air

I am in the air right now
When I should be on earth with you
Drop the ivy robe
I am coming, landing soon
I need to enchant your skin
Gather your secret
Pass it to my lips

Let us split the other apart
And become eternal again
Take it all off
It makes no difference
If I am not home
I know your fallen fabric
As I fly
Descending with me
Floating down to the ground
Let it pass between our lips

It makes every difference
That I am not there
When your fabric falls
As I descend
Landing miles away
Passed by my lips

II. The Wait

You are strung lights
Framing every doorway ever graced
You walk through magnetic light
All things become light
Waiting for you

The lights themselves brighter than before
They will burn out but you never do

When I saw you between the lights
You became incense
Particulate mystery
Raising itself contusing my sight
All storms become cataracts
Thunderous contracting lengths of time

God your body moves
Fashioned in furnace
Electrically charged
You are always more than light
But never less
Brilliant and bright
Downing your missed image with my sight

III. On the Move

You un-gathered me
You become motivating want
Defining the early morning
Before the sun takes over the sky

I have transcendent thoughts
Studied in the tragic
The shadow of death which follows us all
But now is tasted elation
Tracing your soaked clever
The ridge of corporeality

To hold you un-gathered
Coming unapologetically
The very secret of you
History and life
On the move
The concentrated roaring geometry
All angles riding the edge

The loaves and fishes
Gathered into one
The moment hard and soft
Pant and cry
And the cloak of another kind of sigh

There is no winding cloth
Only covers
Covered as high as houses
Covering us
Loving under cover
Licking and nipping
Little bite of you
Twilight play of gods

The Things . . .

I am between days
Too late to be night
Too early for morning
What I have are the things
In the wait for sleep . . .

The press of your raised hips
Your body instinctually reacts
Your mouth praises your mind
Your lip on lip
The cusping mound
So tight I could whistle

Then there is scent
Is it primal depth of matter
The beginning of time
The end of thought
Raw want
Animal and spirit
All of this on my lips and time
So tight I could whistle

Rub me to the sides of your face
My face
At the smile lines
The hint of our essence

Honey stuck sheer delight
So tight I could whistle

I feel your carefully charged fire
That spark and ire
Your spirit magnetic and untiring
Perfected wildfire
I cannot help uncross my legs
Shaking concaving earth
So tight I could whistle

Still, I think
Of your look in shadow
The way your body line
Drapes and changes the scenery
When you become heaven
The apex on my body
All power and pleasure
Consummating the universe
Gratifying the souled verse
Spellbinding rhythmic race
So tight I could whistle

But it is the pulling apart
How you open yourself
Your hands
Your shape beneath me
This is what remains with me between days
You opened self, made wider
Enraptured worlds of you
Your body and sex and sensuality
Your unmistakable mind
Prisms of passion
This is what remains

What the angels cannot claim
You have me down for the count
So tight I could whistle

What Can I Write?

What can I write
That's not about making love to you?
That is the impossible, the joyless, the untrue
Your contour, your hair, your mind
I am missing the squeezed
Deep sea diving
The wet pearl
Stone hot and cool
Seeking you

Everything is bound up in the impelled lush
Thumbed hush
Pull and prod scented bend
The felled earth
Has fallen all around thinking of you

Your hummingbird ringing around roses
Wanderlust beaming faces
Un-ended want wanting you
Bedding you
Needing the sex of you
Creating through
Night and day
You are my closeness
Close and open me

Thinking of you
Flicked licked and sipped
Bronzed meringue tips
Tripping dance of kisses
Sums of you

If I am dying
Why wouldn't I want the memory of your hold
Your finger dance midnight beams easing and rocking
Into things other than death
The life of you
Your sticky sweet and sacred caravan of reverie

Split Apart

God bathes on the top of your tongue
Glass candy yellow red
Liquified soothsaying
Decadent salvation
Bodily praying

Your hands
Drawn warmed feathering
Your touch
Shattering into intervals of anticipation
You part me perfectly

I could not crave your body more
Right now
Right when the sun sinks down
Purple cape of lowered light
Divination in the deep of your time
Growling incarnations chase and align
Crown the night
Long long waiting line
Landscapes after landscapes of you

Search me out, make your demands
Turn me over upside down
There are so many lands between us
I wish you were here

Voyeur of slow motion
Your ineluctable image flow
Irresistible thievery
Wreathing your sighs

I could not crave you more
When the moon is at its peak
Shining black sheet
The unspoken word of your anatomy
The word of your soul
The word of your spirit
Descending on me
I wish you were here

It Is Raining

It is raining here lover
And I am always in the thought of you
The night is late
Morning approaches
I lay stretched on my bed
Alone happy
Thinking of you

Tonight I had my wildness
My running thoughts
The intensity of moving body union
That only you can give
I cannot forget
But I need to remember

I love the humor of you
Now time stretches between us
I know myself pulled close
It remakes me
So in love with your laughter
The power of your convictions
Your sensitive soul
That resides beneath it all
You are softer than soft passage
And stronger than steel
You are eternal and most real

You have made a place for me
Miles in your heart
Living on your embrace
Raining racing to you
Exquisitely loved
Hidden wisdoms
I know and do not know
Your heart knows
Your beauty tones my heart
I hardly know what to do or say

Overcome with your love
All the rain could collect
And it would never be enough

I need to make love to you
To touch your body, kiss your skin
To feel you again
I cannot forget
But I need to remember

All the rain collected
And it would never be enough

Tonight Will Be the Thought of Your Hips

Tonight will be the thought of your hips
The way you can claim the whole bed
Just by sitting on the edge
A world shrouded in your grace
The way you exhale in final prayer

With you I will not be afraid of any terror by night,
nor of the arrow that flies by day

When I am with you
I will drink the water from your glass
Melted snow becoming intercessions
And everything that can transform follows its course

With you I will not fear the pestilence that stalks in darkness,
nor of the sickness that destroys at noonday

Dip into me
Make me yours
The ancient compline
The sanctuary of Zion
When you press the edge of my body
Fusing your silhouette with mine
It is all yours every time

With you though a thousand fall at my side and ten thousand at my right hand, yet it shall not come near me

Tonight is the thought of your hips
The thirty-three stacked vertebrae
The way you claim the world sitting on the edge
A love shrouded in final prayer
The sanctuary of your perpetual care

The Drum

When I become your drum for your percussion formed by your hand
Use the wood of the white poplar tree with buds of caramel and amber scent
Downy clouds doused in oriental perch ready to be nipped by your finger pull

Stabilize me in any mold that encircles your stretched mystique
Soon you will compress the life inside my shell
Heated until the wood is rounded and every piece held is parallel
Keep my frame tight and close always ready for you

When you pull the skin taut across the head, pressing and changing my shape
Silk into envy, greed into brightly dyed wool
I will be your drum
Nothing more and nothing less than your open smooth surface
A crater lake of untrained reflection awaiting the wire brush
Shivering crisp echo
Leaves leaded with cold will fall

When the vibration of my head shakes the silence off your sleeved sex
Percusses the entire drum
Strikes my feature until vibrations dampen becoming the scene
Then the dips and the dives
Then this howled animal will diminish the setting sun

Thirst: The Shared Poems of Artist Carol Scott & Caitlin Smith Gilson

The Goblets, by Carol Scott

Bodies Go Fire

Passion is a palpating band
The carnal lust enshrined
Stretched to the breaking point

We must remain inside its orbit or not
But every wave is pouring
From weakened sides crashed
A pushing and a prying
The contained and the released
The keeping tight and relaxed as untied lace

Smiling lust and galloping joy, shooting across the bed, bodies go fire

To be in your passion is to contract and to extend
Every moment is the one moment transfixed in crystal
The inner thigh quivering slick kiss
At the ridge and the hint of the shave
Skimmed across my face

Your fingers transform to liquid chords
You enter with a singing touch
Pitched high and low
If this is heaven let me live and let me die

Smiling lust and galloping joy, shooting across the bed, bodies go fire

The Severing in Three

I. Soothe

There is a severing into the substance of every life
A cutting open and a pouring in

For a while we are between the release and the taking

At every single moment
If I could tell you the sweet words
The ones that play and soothe

The stand in
The embrace of you
When it is cold
Water turns to rain
Rain turns to ice

When the relentless elements mar the surface of your earth
Forever birdsong
Where the air is scented with flowers
Tears are measured in grief weighted by the love felt in life

II. Submerge

Your hands moving through the blonde
My hair pulled to its side

Submerging my face in yours
I cannot help myself

History making
We have been and are being
Forsaken for us
Lust for the taking
Pleasure merry making
Swimming in gin
Love intoxication

Why should I help myself
Help yourself to me
Eternity
It is now and you are mine
My skin was bruised and now it heals
Glory, glory, glory
Holy is our time together
I find you
The atoms of my soul
The truth of me
Stringing parts into heaven

III. Combust

Whatever split apart in me has become new
When you entranced and threw my center down
Sighing my life into spells
Dancing sliding reanimation
Suspended before falling
I could die

Resurrected in your shimmering
Thrusting loving pushed and plied
Living beguiling piloting thighs
These are the atoms of our soul
Combusted we explode

Then the fallout in the flow of kisses
Each the unlike and multiplied
God you created a beautiful world
Love personified by love
Everything dipped into you
Drink of my drink
Twist of my heart
Squeezed ecstasy
As tears from the blind
Drops of fire on my tongue

New Life

You have been on my mind
I watch the light reflect on the water
And I think of you

In a few hours nature changes
The tidewater governs my legs
And I think of you coming upon me
Your body over mine
Bestriding magnificence

What I know
Is that I never want you out of my mind
I want to think of you
When the water feels like linen
When the waves die down
When the sun is at its last peak
Before it dips into night
Your lips enthralling mine

Thinking now of what I can kiss
The wetness of my mouth
All your sides bathed in mine
When the sun is at its last peak
When it dies down
Undercover
Dripping diamonds

Pink striations
Orange bands across the sky
You have been on mind all day
All night

New bold gold
Old is over
Peaked magnum of magic
Naked music
Free form holding
Pure touches
Perfect fingers and hands
Sempre on my mind
Always burning in memory

The Songs of Solomon

All your downed pearls
All you into me freed
Pink liquid lips
Speaking parted heat
Magnet pull of magic making

All my upward gold
All me into you
Spiraling labyrinthine need

I am what I am . . .

Ransacked
Butterflied snap
Spread buzzing animal greed
Forever the inner read

You are what you are . . .

Tendon stretching
Echolocating homing reprising creed
Ever-perceiving touch trembling me

We are what we are . . .
Boundless brimming besting beckoning body on body

Days with you
Hours with you
Time with your body
The unmarked eon
Your cooing singularity
These things are the downed white pearl
Fingering each bead
Oh . . . sweet
How sweet

Golden upward swing
Surfeited sweet tonic
Ringing body
Honeysuckle drunk silk
Slung fruit of the earth eaten lap
Lingering tectonic scent
Trapped
Packed
Aromatic red cedar sap

Dipping serendipity
Sirens of destiny
Haunting born infinity
Tripped up conjured
Wet whistled veiled lip
Smoldering bunker of fire
Finger slip
Rolling inside
Your Grecian margarite

We are what we are . . .
Lucid liquefying laced lightning life on life

Take me to bed
You think we can survive
This timebound beat of heart
The absent heat

Take me to bed
You think we can survive
The downed ember
The unfinished start

Take me to bed
You think we can survive
The sucked-up starless night
The final light

I will crawl
Instead of speak
Week broken week
Recollected walk
Your body
My body
Peak into valley and peak

The who of us
The what of us
Why is obvious
Lovely love lust

Loving you
Circulates the air
Moves my blood
Loving you
Makes lullabies of my sleep
Smoked mesquite

Shined ruby on velvet black
Loving you

One Liners

Your smile is so good it crisscrosses time
I feel it at my door, in my step
Enjoy me

Your touch flawless
We have melted into one
I see you and I adore
Please me

I am tumbling in your heat
Your presence is kindling
Our tongues are flame
Drink me

I lap the dew
Sipping, sucking, combusting
Have me

Enjoy my shallow
Salt my surface
Play at my depth
Enter my hallow
Food of me

Feast of sight
Perpetual pleasure

Every morsel cherished
Till we are done

The Story of a Soul

Since when did you become all fire?
Burning in your wake
Waves of shivering searing kicks of flame
Igniting my soul

My body stamped with fire
Red wax seal
Doused and drenched
You have me grinding earth into fire
Riding high
Your soul match-stroke inferno

Sway me raid me back and forth
Divinely mad spirit
Set alight burning bright
Invading pleading howling your name!

Give me time I will never tire
Pricked heat
Too beautiful too good
The story of a soul
Soaring restoring
Firestorm of you burned through me

Perhaps you were born ablaze
But who could survive?

If you play with fire, you are surely to burn
Hot, hot, hotter
Streetcar named desire
Tabasco delicious
Smiling lips of midnight kisses
Thrusting hips of a noonday run
Galloping legs
Burn baby burn
You are my match

VI

It Is Finished

There is death in life, and it astonishes me that we pretend to ignore this: death, whose unforgiving presence we experience with each change we survive because we must learn to die slowly. We must learn to die: that is all of life. To prepare gradually the masterpiece of a proud and supreme death, of a death where chance plays no part, of a well-made, beatific, and enthusiastic death of the kind the saints knew to shape. Of a long-ripened death that effaces its hateful name and is nothing but a gesture that returns those laws to the anonymous universe which have been recognized and rescued over the course of an intensely accomplished life. It is this idea of death, which has developed inside of me since childhood from one painful experience to the next and which compels me to humbly endure the small death so that I may become worthy of the one which wants us to be great. I am not ashamed, my Dear, to have cried on a recent early Sunday morning in a cold gondola which floated around endless corners through sections of Venice only so vaguely visible that they seemed to branch out into another city far away. The voice of the barcaiolo who called out to be granted passage at the corner of a canal received no answer, like in the face of death. And the bells that I had heard in my room only moments before (my room where I have lived a whole life, where I was born and where I am preparing to die) seemed so clear to me; those same bells dragged their sounds like rags behind them over the swirling waters only to meet again without any recognition. It is still always that death which continues inside of me, which works in me, which transforms my heart, which deepens the red of my blood, which weighs down the life that had been ours so that it may become a bittersweet drop coursing through my veins and penetrating everything, and which ought to be mine forever. And while I am completely engulfed in my sadness, I am happy to sense that you exist, Beautiful. I am happy to have flung myself without fear into your beauty just as a bird flings itself into space. I am happy, Dear, to have walked with steady faith on the waters of our uncertainty all the way to that island which is your heart and where pain blossoms. Finally: happy.

—Rainier Maria Rilke, *The Dark Interval*

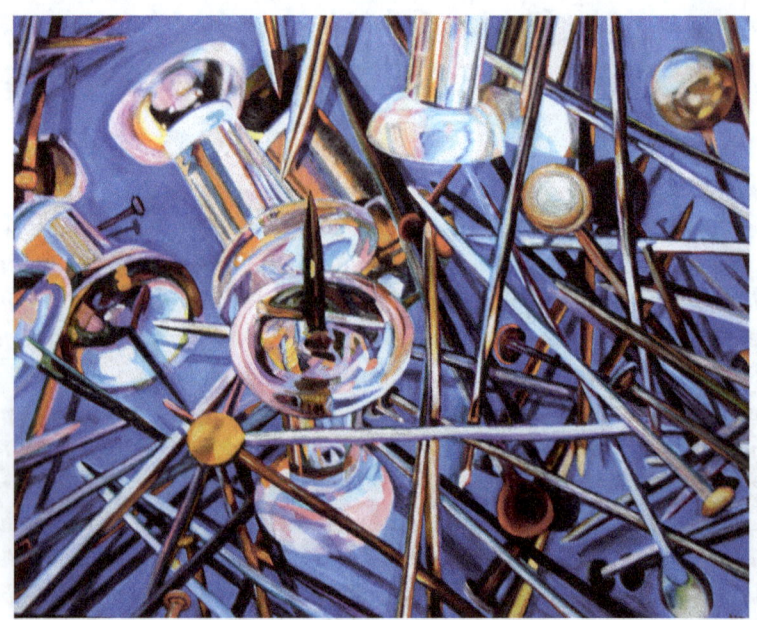

Pinned and Pricked, **by Carol Scott**

The Velveted Cape

The velveted cape of your voice
Comes from far away and next to me
Sounds long descended
Into the cold of my breathing

Your voice is the originating myth
The stab of the spirit
Plunders my heart
This heart which will stop someday

Your voice is the kind of time
That breaks the world
You
Your speaking
Your being
Have marked the first and last time . . .

My heart stops dead in its rhythm
Restarting itself by sheer desire
The sound of you naming me

Your voice is my love for you
The force of my body
Becomes stretches of sun
Over tides of stilled water

Way beyond sound
I hear your voice and I smile

When the waves parted
The water turned into cloth
Oh God, is this my time of dying?

Evensong

The evensong of your hair
Moonless descending raven
All over the black linen
Each lock
An all-knowing messenger
Exhaling the background

All I can comprehend is your face
Your shimmering shapeshifting
Figurations in gliding sable
Each finger placed and replaced
In the ebbing current

Your hair sinking into the pillow
Read into the firmness of the bed
Gazing into inkwells
Just this sight will bring me to expiration

If I survive this image
Bathed in the River Styx
Your layers of sea silk metamorphoses
Then I will become invulnerable
Except for one dip
One niche
One strawberry incarnation
Only you will know

And you will feel me
In my descent
That when touched
I am instantly freed

When we are done being lovers
Let us be lovers again
Take the fresh dates
Out of the airtight container
One after another
Bite to the stone
Elliptical and grooved
Skipping across surfaces
Sweet ineluctable honey
Sticky caramelized depth

What Else Can I Say

What else can I say
I love you
I did not know
I could love the way you take me apart
And make me more

This is not because of lack of love
I have loved much
I could survive the sun
I can melt myself and become anew

The life of my children my family
Of touch, oceans of touch
Of their sweetness that conjures the fierce and the soft
I am all these things even when I enter the grave

When we see the stars now
What is in the present is already past
These lights faded away thousands of years
Before any one of us entered the grave

But you
You are every single sun
That ever was and ever will be
I do not survive you

I desire you in my desire being desired
Disintegrating in your love

My heart is glossed texture
You would barely notice if it touched your perfect face
Your lips
And you took me into you
And we became what we are

I love you with the God in me
I have survived the sun
You always will be
Every star of all stars desired

Your release is the complete
This crushes the glass of me
A collision of being and time itself

We cannot love another completely
We cannot love what we do not know
That is the paradox of loving God

All the regions we do not see
To feel this pain on earth
In every entered and neglected grave
To grasp the beloved and fall short
We cannot wrap them entirely
And all joys carry a shadow of this
Of the failure to know and to love

But you love me beyond memory
Why would I survive your love?

The Jewelry Box

My rib cage is the jewelry box of my heart
The place of my spirit
Which I breathe in and out
This is all that I am
A life

When I sleep these bones stretch and descend
When I wake stretching and descending
Sealed and unsealed rosebud under glass
This is my heart inside its shell
A concert of tendons covering
The bronzed cage of the bell
This comprises me
I am flesh and blood
A life unremarked
My life in time

My heart is the light
Inside its beacon made of bone
This is me
A body among many
Breathing
Blood coursing to my mind and my legs
The warmth and pressure in my fingertips as I write
I feel my bones over my heart
It is

I am
You are
The inner rhythm
Of your paper lantern
Bright colors resting on mine

This is love
To be living body
A luminescence in the lighthouse
Flashing out to sea for decades
I am in the place of flesh made for my spirit
At the center of my chest
The bone becomes solid
An armor over my heart between my breast
Softness relenting into the firm
A firmament of muscles
Contracting under my skin
Touching the origin of time

If you move your hands
Over the ridges of my bones
You will be where I am
Where I breathe in and out my life
I was born to breathe until the last day
God, someone hold me

This is all I am
A work of art
A life breathing
Bones sewn to bones
The sacred alone
One body hewn from stone
I feel my bones over my heart
It is

I am
You are
The inner rhythm
Of your light resting on mine

The Image

Images are everything
They come before the word
Images survive the ravages of age
They inebriate the angel

Images live above meaning
Freed from necessity
They animate the mind
They are the hidden cord

Your sheer untouched body
Descending to my face
Your genesis
The alighting image
Inebriating the angels

The image is meaning-giver
The risen breathing being
Colliding image
The everything

The image of your sheer untouched body
My face
The shifted world
A continuum of my hands
Pulling you down into my image

Images of your perfect control
Rocking the held headboard
Images of undiluted motion
The metric of your dance

Images of your peeled open body and soul
Rising and crumbling
Shivering bands, the bed of ships
Images of your second coming
Your sheer untouched body
Descending

Images are God sheathed in skin
Images are unarranged cadence
Images inebriate the angels
Your image is everything

The Wordless Said

What is the quiet exactly
That we need for sleep
That we need?

I can still hear the singer's voice
Rising and falling
Foreign and sealed
Italian poetry
The room turned into trees
Infinite trees
One day burning inside us

How much more life
Do we give
Do we receive?
How much more I do not know

A life died today
Rising and falling eternity
Random life filled with heartbreaking randomness
These entwined patterns too intricate to see
Random to you and to me
To give and to receive

I could die tomorrow
Fail to wake

True to know this dying
To claim things passing
My body ages
Wanting what it wants
To be kissed, covered again
To hear you rising and falling
Infinite tree
Infinite memory
Burning

What is the quiet exactly
That we need for sleep
That we need?

All I know is that I need you asleep
Next to me
That is the quiet
That is the need
Given and received
Burning up in me the wordless said

At this moment
I am walking the path to the water again
I doubt I will see a soul between the dunes
Rising and falling

Families congregating in the cafes in sun
Sunday drawn
The Basilica soon to sound its bells
Somewhere the sound of your touch hides
Swells of the sea

How much more of life
Do we give

Do we receive
How much more I do not know

Children running in circles
Collapsing and rising
In this dying October
Soon to be winter
Nothing more than my footfall and the waves
Listening to the space below voices
My body in time
Silence inside silence
Infinite burning trees
Nothing more than the silence
The space between voices
The feeling of you
The wordless said

Stratosphere

You
Flow as current
Shot through the stratosphere
Raining down from high altitude
Disarming thought
A series of single vowels
Word is everything

Your body
Its own depth of force
Against me

Next time I see you
Unchained satin
Final curtain
Body and blood
Brought close

You
Making you the end of me

The God of Inscape

My heart has hit the pavement
Broke open
No blood, all water
Squeezed into your high relief and drunk
Sun risen sheen of your conception
Intrinsic creation
Works of passionate infinity
Collapsed into your art
My heart

You must do the feeling for me
I am loving you with my broke-open heart

My senses implode with your lift and fall
Brush stroke concupiscent arrow
Rioting insight
Castles cast
You are nuclear fission in flesh
The indrawn form
The laid out vacant object inscape light
Quantum tunneling energetic cut and dash
Rile and caress the thermogenic red
Ripped covers of the lover's bed
I am all water no blood
Washed in your palette

Collapsed into your art
My heart

You must do the feeling for me
I am loving you with my broke-open heart

I submerge my soul into newly fallen snow
Pigmented stained line
Reverberated time
You turned me into tears
At the very drop of your voice
Your art is word
Anchoring lake of beauty
The imaged verb
Undress the lowdown sound
Echoing love
Lanced with light
Raided with shade
Collapsed into your art
My heart

You must do the feeling for me
I am loving you with my broke-open heart

At first sight you laced me up
Sipped up nectar of your face
A place perceived
A homeland received
A phantom risen incense breathed
Your rhythmic shoulders
Reigning above me in bowed shadow
Do the feeling for me
Stretched wood of my waiting
Codas of longing

Colliding with your felt image
Sockets drawn and redrawn
Raised and erased and raised into your form
Collapsed into your art
My heart

My lover
My dearest lover
You must do the feeling for me
I am loving you with everything I am
I am loving with my broke-open heart

My Dream

I plan to love you as you *should* be loved
You form light into life majestic

My desire for you is the exotic in the familiar
The familiar in the unknown
The water in the desert
The feeling that feels for you
Drills deep into meaning
In all your sweet dreaming

In other words . . .

I plan to love you as you *should* be loved
You break sight into truth and beauty

My swept up entirety needs you to create
With all the love there ever was
Every corner in every home of every earth
All that love recreated

I plan to figure out the mystery of life and lay it at your feet
That way everything good
Pours back into you

When I make love to you
I am pouring out

I am practicing the world of love
Overflowing

I wish you to accomplish
The impossibly good
The impossibly true
The impossibly beautiful
I need you to create love beyond me

That is my dream

The Lottery

In the realm of probabilities
You are the lottery
The one in one billion chance
The boundless being and dance

The remains of heaven
Have animated your honeyed marrow
Motionless ecstasy
Divinizing your studied feature
Numberless eyes
Sliding into lower mantle
And volleying from the sky

You have me
Plummeting from tin space shuttle
Buried alive
Drawn and erased and drawn again
This is more than nature
It is the re-creation
Quartz in quicksand
Soon to be struck glass

Bound two-bodied griffin
If you depart I could not die
I would have no heart

You are the metamorphic rock
Hurled before time

You strike every chord
The instrument of my body
Tempest of vital force
The song-land of play
Perpetual verse
The final act
The fractured curse
Forever Sunday

In the night's canopy
The body of the deities
Pinpricks of light
Scattered beyond the telescope
Past the strongest material sight
All iron and steel and titanium
All impenetrable unbroken lens
But you pushed farther and father still
To be the gamble itself

Too Tired to Dream of Cities

Too tired to dream of cities
Large vacant windows
Never letting in the light

But I can think of you
Straddling this quaking body
Willing maker life-taker

Somewhere around the fall
But before the rising seas
You became the myth of the sky
Unaware of the ground below
Untouched by the advent of time

There is no one who could resist
Your unstudied ecstasy
Altar of silence and lore
Chimera of sunlight and love

The Last Faith

It was gradual and sudden
The shiver of the tree splintering
That aching caress of angles
When the inside is finally hit
I always thought the center would hold

It was there in my sleeping
I did not approach the entity
The wreathed garland of my keeping

The wood cracks unable to withstand
The causation of its own mass
The sound of the cut
Weighted echoes in shafts of silence
Wailing without response
Time of no mind
Time of bravery unto death
For none listen longer than you

I thought it would take longer to fall
I did not know Lover of Threes
I would be sliced away
A bloodless idea
A vacant riddled organism cleaved
That throb and terribly lonely need

That caress of sheared angles
It was then I learned I lost my faith

Tell me it is not you God
It is not you
I cannot believe and I do not doubt you
Come back to me
I thought the center would hold

My lost faith
Wailing fractured form without response
Disembodied and breaking
Cracked cypress and pine
Wooden splintering time of your Cross
Unable to take my fall

Finished: The Shared Poems of Artist Carol Scott & Caitlin Smith Gilson

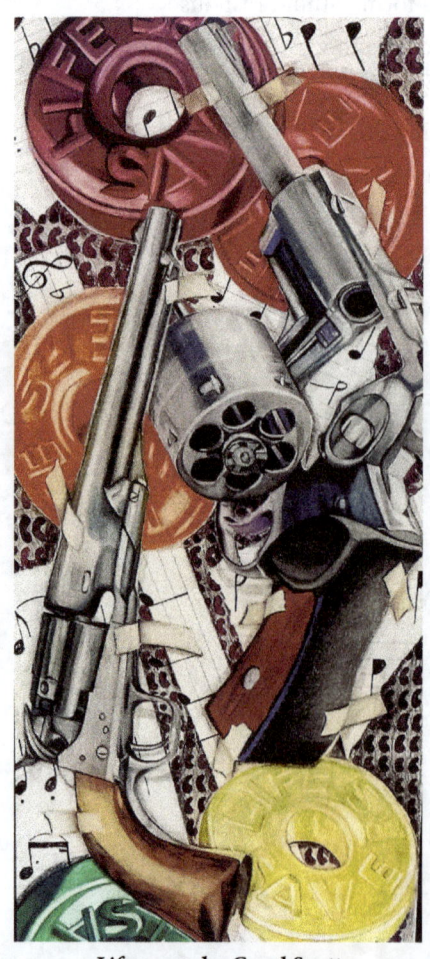

Lifesavers, by Carol Scott

The Eros of the Risen Lord

Down me as last drink before the desert
I am the very substance that will keep you alive
Time is time is time
There is no mistaking what it means to be in time
Your birth is your death
Knee depth in dunes of blown sand and heat
Breadth of earth soon your bones
I am Eros
God of the alone

How can I know you?
Where can I find you?

Blinding sun swallowed flight
Phoenix un-resurrected pale and white
Unwrap my sheet
The stone must bleed
Time is time this time of need
The fruit of your withered seed
I am Eros
God of the host

When can I receive you?
Is it time?

You are dying
Flightless wages of the age
Sugar cane rot your teeth
But I am the drink
The sinking soul
The body cold
I am Eros
God of the call

Did I hear you?
Is it time?

I am your intoxicant
Immunity from pain and death
Your guard against the lie
The final universal cry
Aged amber cognac decanted
Gilded lost dream redeemed
Drink me
I am Eros
God of flesh and bone

Did you create me?
Is it time?

Your body
Beneath the surface
Shimmering white rum
Scent of ocean
You can have me the sum undone
Every cloud condensed
Made into form
Crushed grapes transformed
Consume me

I am Eros
God of sun and moon

Where can I find you?
Are you in the tomb?

Don't you realize I drank you long ago
I can live on nothing
Make the fantasy of rain suffice
Substantialize pain into sweet river
Out of vice
The rain floats before it falls
Tapping my tongue
Fields of rice grown in flooded rows of water
I am the thrice vision
The cycle of life
The sensual the mystical the confession
The holy night
Permeating every lifeless shadow
The sensual call
The incarnate reverie
Down me in your mind
Draw me in your lips
Devour me in your heart
I am Eros
God of your body and soul

Are you coming?
Are you in the tomb?

Playing life and death
Unbridled desire for union
Penetrating oneness
God of eternity and light

Flowering divine
God of sacraments and sacrifice
When my time has ended
When it is done
Call me to eternity
Eros and union
Love of the Risen Lord

Are you the bread of my body?
Are you in the tomb?

If You Could See Me

If you could see me wrapped in a towel
As orange as risen sun
Hair wet
Body tired
Wondering where you are

If you could see me curled in its companion sheet
Resting in the few moments
Before life
Jotting lines
Things are brighter than fresh squeezed juice
I have yet to hear the bells mark the time

This day must begin
I wonder where you are
I think of you in the depth
Within the silent parade of night
Passing over and through

I am cut with electric color
Somewhere you sleep in the cool black of dark and shadow
Healing your body
Resting your soul
Perhaps a shooting star passed your way?
Perhaps an animal howled for you?

Rest is good, work is good, love is best
Different places
Even time not the same
Routine unshared

I wonder where you are
This world on borrowed time
Devoured lengths
Stretched past any human life
There is the beyond existing before me
Rolling on filled in destiny

At midday
I wondered about you and walked into time
Perhaps the sun has passed your way?
Perhaps the rain too?

My hair dried in the bright air
Miles of sky above and stone below
Sculpted elegies in marble
Fathers and sons
Fingers bent
All of this
Existing before you
Before me
In the aftermath of the living
Down to the breached apple core

Today I touched a wall formed before Christ was born
Hidden in the basement of a library
Too many faces lost
I placed my hand
The wall cannot withstand my time
Little by little breaking

Things crumbling
Falling apart
Changing
I wonder where you are in all of this
This time bound time
Ineluctable stretch down the line
Devouring everything

Rest is good, work is good, love is best
Different places
Even time not the same
Routine unshared

Even if I know how to find you, I am still searching
Waking for you
Looking into the ether
Wondering which star shot past you in the night
I placed my hand
Time cannot withstand

How good to hear your voice
I wondered where you were
Today the sound of you shot through my body
Into destiny
The soul of me
As if my ear was made of your voice

In the late afternoon on the footbridge
Looking out at the river to St. Peter's
All light pierced the clouds
Little by little things changing
Crumbling
Remade

I think you stretch beyond any human life
I wonder always where you are

Are you as near as a memory
Touching reality
Hugging, smiling
Always talking?

Cannot Stop

Snowfall
Without you
You never go unnoticed
You drift in and out of me
And the earth gives up its ghost

Ten thousand hours
You have what it takes
Star worked polished
Shadows on the wall
Faith fulfilling prophecy
Still here
My ghosts are with me
Embraced by my past
Carrying my dead
Integrity in the hewn rock
Futility in greatness

My sacred contract
Trust hovers over
Confetti raining gifts
Life

We Are Swimming between Universes

We are swimming between universes
You are cosmic shift
The prayer
The sign
The bang of light
Burst open landmine
Life bringer
Tossing me into fire
Inebriated drink of the well of time
Universe of mine

If nothing of me remained
I would still love the salt of you
The anything
The everything
That survived the death of minds

When I burn up
Disintegrate
Passing through atmosphere
Caressing you
Hurtling down
I will hear your voice
The sound of water
Passing through my riverbed
Universe of you

Completing you
Amplifies sound
Condenses silence
Pleasures the abyss
Refines thought
Reified life bringer
Fire giver
Immersed in water moments before the ice of winter
You are inside and outside
Pulling me
Bright and dark
Breathing urgency
All universe and intimacy
Terrifyingly beautiful
Universe of mine

All my sun and moons multiplying
Dividing into singular image
Your face at the door
Your head on my breast
The one stilled glimpse
Moving through me
Universe of you

Orbits experiencing gravity
This trajectory
Inescapable and haunting
I feel your pull
Halving
Merging
Gutting
Subduing
Loving
I feel your pull bring me down on these knees

Across the leagues of spirit and soul
Wave breaker
Our universe of yours and mine

Cliff diving
My exhilarated body plunges into your excitement
Undivided with the ocean
Pounded and carried by the waves
Tides following the moon
As water grows deeper
Splitting apart
Moaning till the rotation comes around
Ego eclipsed into a ring of fire
Ecstasy dancing

Happy
Backstroking
Floating
Resting in our love
Floating between universes

Today Is the Day of All

Today is the day of all
The seizing passion
Beauty in the play of life and death
Gating through the heavens

Hours alone with You
Days poured into You
Attention, endurance, patience
Exquisite rigorous care
Built cathedral of my life

Work is the God
Work is the prize
Work is the North Star

Eyes do not fail
Back do not tire
Hands remain steady
I give my love all that I am
Always ready to receive You
Eternal life and legacy await
Wrapped as bond around my heart

You are magnetizing joy
Bubbling from my skin
Embracing spiked delight

Pure light
A sparkling divinity

Your love comes upon me
It comes upon my soul
All its colors
All its canvased light
All mercy and life
All exotic blues
Adorning me
Un-perishing
Lived again
Today is the day of all

My love is the God
My love is the prize
My love is the North Star

There is a beauty in starting to work
First step
Diving in
Promise of an end
Dancing with anxiety
Prevents progress
Once begun

Work is the God
Work is the prize
Work is the North Star

One foot in front the other
Millions of strides
Large and small
Trillions of walks

Through the forest
Up the mountain
In the swamp
Gating through the heavens
Full spectrum or blindness dark

I give my love all that I am
Always ready to receive you, art
Eternal life and legacy await
Wrapped as bond around my heart

Work is the God
Work is the prize
Work is the North Star

VII

Father, into Your Hands I Commend My Spirit

Whenever He looks at you, God sees nothing in us that He has not given. Everything is empty until He places what He wishes into it. The soul is like an uninhabited world that comes to life only when God lays His head against us. The delight a child can know tossing a ball into the air, my Lord confessed He experiences whenever He looks at you. God sees nothing in us that He has not given.

—St. Thomas Aquinas, *Whenever He Looks at You*

Chandelier in Pink, by Carol Scott

The Winter's Allegory

In this Winter's allegory
Deep pines and velvet reds masking our shadows
The snow is falling but we are a furnace
Every snowdrop detonates instantaneously
I catch sight of my breathing
My spirit slipping past me into you

Even in night
In the shortest days of the year
We are bodies in motion
Respiring automatically
Some one thing takes over
When we forget
This breathing
This remembering you in the now
Ceaseless inhaled life
Reanimating my blood
Tonic of being
The moment of birth
The closing of the book

This breathing is the keeping
Rounding Saturn's rings
Lonely deep midnight of breathing
The sidewinding shadow of you

Cast across my lethargy
Inner solstice of still air

I cannot conceive
Barren imageless spirit
Balletic now broken respiration
Brought in and out
How I breathed when I learned she died
When we know the color loss
The bodies which end
Tender
Surrender
Cost and cost
Their motion
The ages, the age in the air
How could I breathe that day
In the spectacle of the fallen form
Reasonless breathing of being and time

Love is spiritual food and drink
It is the age-old elegy of yearning
Immortality in the drawn breath
The you of me
Wreaths of purpled berries and greenery
The breathing recaptured
Raptured inhaled souls
Fed on air
Ransoming the gods

All ends and codas
The whole head must turn
To inhale air that wallops
A form of expiration
Air vibrating into spindles

Impaling the heart nearing the lungs
I breathe the faraway getaway taste
Of the salt I miss
I mistake the rhythm of your breathing
Heart-aching ways of oceanic breathing

All the snowdrops crowding around
Evaporating into air and heat
Breathing you into decades of me
You underlie the in and out
Of your bodied spirit
Lunging bodies without fatigue
Remembering and forgetting

To breathe again
Breathing the spirit
The falling asleep in breathing
The furnace of your body
The firmament of our embrace

To circulate life as the days before
The days after
Long after
Shadowless notes
Blown into the breeze
Forgetful breathing
Dreamland of love
Breathing
Baking the air

In the Final Month

We never quite feel
The satellites puncture the atmosphere
Rings of violent steam
Descending into the Atlantic
Defeated without playing any game

Nor do we know
The dying of deep-rooted things
Vines as thick as wheels of fate cut down

There are gallons of vacant expression
Unwashed by feeling
Poured alongside our every walk
Trenches of ice
Fueled with prehistoric death
Careening towards the basic element

We navigate little with little
The crust of bread
The bitter types of ends

Somewhere I am
Paddling up the waterfall
That are my bones
Turning out their marrow

There is a world rocking itself into oblivion
Miles of souls shelved and waiting
Lost below the earth
Tell me, love
This is not for us

I cannot feel a time before
My blood was warm
Before blood was shed
Before altars and sacrifice
All of me
Whatever I am is yours

There are deserts of dead planets circling us
Yet they fit inside a single thought
This complexion of moving things
It will be our death
Still all of you
You are the glimpse

There is so much to this life
There are so few words we have
So few
But I tell you, love
In the final month of the year
Loving you has been the gift

When You Sway the Heavens

When you sway the heavens
And your head relaxes its weight
Falling back
All earth is lost forever
It slips inside your face
Reversed tears
Every ounce inside your eyes

I think you have gone to years before me
Young as bitten peach

Half of you in distant light
The other in the ancient shade that once cast
The world into its first sleep
A puzzle of two pieces
You slip in and out of me
All I can do is breathe out my spirit
Finding the earth beneath your skin

Your life, your life
Your passion
Your pleasure is sacred to me
This is the architecture of my longing
How can I survive?

You have made me from your tears
I am the sea of Galilee
The boats passing brightly
The catch in your nets
The damp of your lips
As the cup passes by
Let the cup pass by
There is no pain here

Oh Holy Christ
There is the word of death
And the word of life
The doors open
The windows
I will never close them
Come to me
Beautiful song
Torched body
Earth of you
I turn into wilderness in your fire

I think you have gone to years before me
Young as bitten peach

You affect my symmetry
The force of your life
I look at your face
Your face says it all

There is no earth
Your happiness is the holy
The earth is gone
Curve your back into the art of my hand
Wrapped completely

Downed world
Dropped cut flowers
Your face veils the sky
Worlds in the broke-open thigh
How can I survive?

Oh Holy Christ
The wheel of chance
The dance of death
Arch my back into the bridge of you
Before the world was made
It slipped inside your face
And I was the waking stream
Let the cup pass by
There is no pain here

I think you have gone to years before me
Young as bitten peach

On the Train

On the train
Transported back-and-forth
Nonstop relentless movement
Tired into the spirit fatigue

I am certain that if you looked at me
The way you do . . .

My eyes are not as bright
The shadow music of the train's whistle
I close my eyes only to catch a break
To enter something other, nothing

It is there that I can feel my lover
The one I love
Your kiss
The weight of it
So very light I think it is
A strand of my own hair falling on my lips
Between waking and sleep
Even this
And I am alive again

The long-opened door
The sound of it
Separating and rejoining

It closes and another stop has passed
Your near absence hovering
The shunting sigh of brakes released

I can barely skate this surface to give you
The gravitational pull of the train bonded to metal track
A vortex lingers between distances
Something in me *happened*
Layers and volleys and images
A structural world reached into the orbit
And made me a body in motion

You have entered in ways I cannot grasp
In sleeping strands on my lips
Haunted line of boxed steel cars waking
Layering volleying imagistic play with the silhouette
In the windows of the train
Say any words any at all and the Song of Songs
Something other
You are
The opened door of another stop

You have pierced through the center with a sword
In some way you extinguished me
So gentle I barely know
That I am transfixed
Affixed to all passing scenery
Out these windows till I am back to you

No one can undress me as you do
I barely know enough
This torrent
These strands on my lips
I thought it was you

My heavy eyes
Flowing through the train

Loving You Makes the Word

Inside the thrown word
There are infinite variations of loving you

Words have ways and means
They lay tightly packed in black-inked bondage
Whipped up storm of word
Your life adored

Stretch your power
Till the next word comes
You are the witching hour
A gliding jet
Subterranean leagues of subtext
I am pulled apart in your coated paper
Falling as snow
Burning the decks
A crimson trail
Cleaving the sea

You are the line from my lips
The pressed together verb
The cast word
Words bring alive the rim of the glass
Thick at the center of your fingertip
Rocks the ice

Words bring alive the compressed base
Faceted cuts harnessed light
The poured forth verve
Clean burning willful sting held over the table
In your perfect nonchalance

Words bring alive your naked silhouette
The winter cold hushed over your body
Turned into spring
Never expired

Words bring alive the *I love you*
Loving you
Wildly longing
Imagining you

You are the only word
There ever was and will be
There will always be
You and me
There will always be
More sacred consecrations to the slope of your back
Squeezed cheeks I hold on for hours
All the way down and through
The promise of my word and tongue

You are the only word that ever was and will be

The Passing Thought

The scent of fresh sea air in Autumn
Has a way of reminding me of you
In spite of the feeling that this chill in sun has a sadness to it
A foreshadowing of winter suns barely strong enough to warm the days
The long dark December nights
Still I am brought into view of you
The passing thought remains within me
You bundled up immune to cold all body warm

The scent of that freshness
The sea close at hand
The bells always on time always a surprise
The sun still beating through the windows
Into the deep of Autumn
All of this has a way of transporting my senses back
Giving all my senses back to you
This passing thought stays within me
For the time being I am looking out at the passing scene
Without my senses yet feeling the everything

How is it that the scent of fresh sea air
In this autumn at this moment
Has a way of reminding me of you?

We never walked the beach together
So many things we have not done

It is enough only to be
Sleep loving sleep
Two presences dreaming for the other
Into the other
All the good giving the good
The sun beating through your window
Into the deep of Autumn
The passing thought sits within me

The height of where I am now
I can take in gallons of that air
I can breathe it in till my lungs tire
Till I am famished
Thinking of warmth

I see the whole town of people passing
The air mixed up in all things
The wind threatening to pull the linen off
The white tables decorated for Sunday lunches
After Mass
Shorter homilies
God we pray
Broken bread dipped in wine
Laughter into the night

I think of late nights
How the later afternoon
Lays down its shoulders into late night
The tablecloths are blowing up and down
Barely fixed to their existence
With well-placed glasses
This scene
The comedy of it
The joy of being

The frenetic need
Has a way of bringing me back to days with you
But more the nights

My toes stuffed now under the covers
Making trenches, blanketed hills
The cold
Come to think of it, it is cold
So many passing thoughts
My limbs separate from my body
The encroaching winter
The sea water has its salt on my skin
My hair drips with it in waves
The thought of hot shower
Eyes closed
Your home
The sense of being between two seasons
This finds me longing for you

On the Way

On the last day
I feel the sky hurtling its heavens
Its cobalt and sapphire
Every time I have loved the sky
Loved the sea
Fallen deep into the sleep of you
All compressed into one
On the last day

In the last hour
I put my feet down into the sand
Time itself collecting me
Repaying my fines
Foreshadowing resignation and sleep
The great dissolution
The eternal dissolve
Which only God can re-collect
On the last hour

In the last moment
Before I lose my name
I hope it is your name on my lips
Breathing you in
Breathing you out
Each syllable particulate matter
Finery

Drawn lace
Long sighs of you
As if your name is an angel
Your name guiding me
In that last moment
When all the pain
All the pandering
All the pleading
Bleeds out
Sinks the sun below the earth
My mind below memory
My children
The smell of their heads
Their pretty little faces
Just the thought
Solidifying my blood
Stopping my heart
The mere sight of them
Inside me
Roads that dip
Cold drink
Cool sip
Autumn waiting for winter
The passion of you
All bound up
These things
The perfumes of my life
The sex, the sweat, the water, the wine
The pressed oil
Scooped out avocado
Delicious sweet cream
Risen steam
You watching me cook
Watching me make a mess

I am watching you sleep
You fall asleep too easily
The curve of you
Dreaming bow at your gates
To drink at your well
The sound of your voice
Long sighs of you
As if your name is an angel
Guiding me
The sound of you
Spoken through mine
In the last moment

The Body of Christ: A Cycle for You

You have become echo
Swirling around my inner sense
Hitting a pitch
I know not how
The sound of you could save me

The floodgates of my crumbled soul
Dissolve
Paper thin
Fireless ash
The cool stilled haunting
Torn open tenderness
Emptied box
The lots of our earths
In the longing I have never known

You are blood and water
Christ in my skin

Pull me back into my skin
Raised from the dead
The chilled stilled haunting
Wilderness of heart
Missing your vision
Coming from the other room

Seeing and being seen
The sight of you could save me

This longing is on my lips
Virginal song of my opened tenderness
Shaking, immolating
The musk of you could save me

You have become reflection
Catching sight of you in the glimpse
The glossy wet stone
Worlds fading from view
The theatrical curtain velvet drop
Only you
Cooler motionless haunting
Craterous heart
Stamped out of my shadowlands

Christ consumed
Christ in us
Christ as we wake
Christ as we sleep

Why do we need to enter the other?
Feel the body of the other?
Its wild spring
Its biological imprint
Hearted crimson drop
The hidden fortress of you
Stopped in my track
I think of you salvaging me
And my head falls back
The colder unmoved haunting
Torn open tenderness

Where else do we find meaning?
In making love there is a hidden boundary crossed
The impossible collision
Union debriding distance
To feel what you are and more
To love what you are and more
This sense I do not know
But I know it could save me
How can we understand without submersion?

My kisses want your body to be water
My sunk head into your waist
Watching your face watch me
Watching your head fall back submerged into the pillow
The look of you could save me

Christ on my face
Christ in your kiss
Christ as wine
Christ as my lips

The world is covered in earth
Places to bury the dead
Even the sun descends
The touch of you is worthy of every death
I want to pass into you
How else is there meaning?
We cannot know but we must be
Pull yourself open for me
Moving and haunting
My gaping heart on the floor

My mouth wants your body to be water
Your muscles to separate

How else is there any meaning?
We cannot know but we must be
The braille of me and I the braille of you

Blood and Water
The eternal wine
Entering you
The savage ravaged sweeter mysticism
One true act
Coinhering the beloved
I give you my body-stained soul
All my tears taste of salt and water
Your salt preserves the felt body
Love is more than life

My soul is your body in water
When I pass into you
Your hand on my breasts
My face so far back only my jaw seen
There is no other meaning but creation loved
Loving you
Passing into you
I give you my blood-stained soul
Torn open tenderness
The touch of you could save me

Christ Jesus
My Christ
Our Lord and Lamb
Savior of body and soul

The Everything About You

It is the everything about you
No one else comes close
My heart is your playground
All reserves too
Everything left
Every combination of my spirit
Of my beginning and my now
At sunset's end

My spirit craves the kind of death which makes it whole

My body would starve for days waiting
If it was a choice between the *now* of buttered hot bread
Or the *days later* licked honeydew
My body would always choose you

My body wants to rest
Sleep through the night with you
Feel the fold of you
Arm around arm around arm around arm
Somewhere between it all
A mix of legs and chests and backs
But most of all your face
Your face the rhyming couplet
Next to mine

All verse
Deepest eyes

My body craves the kind of death which makes it whole

I sing for your rest, your sleep, your fold, your arm, your face
Always your face

If it was the choice between the *today* of sun and ocean
Or the *weeks later* of reading with you
Bet on my endurance
Bet on dying too

Do you know what loss can do?
How it rises from the ground
Weighted watery shoe
Sunk into the marsh
Missing my soul
Missing the soul of you

My soul has come to the place of no return
Cycles and cycles
Countless swinging soulless doors
No exit
Trapped floors

My soul craves the kind of death which makes it whole

My senses need to live
To leap from cliff, to fly
They tire too easily
Wax sugar comb
Honeybee

Sunless tracks desert bloom
Sand clenched teeth
Splintered feet
Relentless dogmatic priority
This is it
This is all there ever was
Haunted by sensations of greed

My sensation craves the kind of death which makes its whole

I will stay in silence
Withered on the vine
Lose my feeling
My sight
My hearing
Cut it all out
Faded peeling wall
Of grated sound
Miles of lifelessness
'Till I gain my peace

I crave you, the kind of death which makes me whole

Rolled in Lotus

My soul is at your words
Shipwrecked
The cool and the wet
Rolled in green
Wrapped to be set
Stone carved basin
Filled with touch
Ready for the cut

This is death
The one act
The claiming
And your eyes
Always your eyes
Impenetrable sable
Measuring my descent

One moment I was gone
The next you had me
The untouched veil
Spiraling to the ground
Stabs of purpled folds
Shafts of golds and greens
The present rolled in lotus

You are
The Kiss and the Word
The kerosene
The followed verb
The storehouse of my sensation

On the Hillside

Why can't we rummage the sky
Some fanciful image that captures
Something that is not
Nor ever will be
This shooting a life into starlight

Why can't we live the single day
Drinking honey mixed with heat
Risking the wide and deep
Black wells and peaks
That turn tonight into you
Yes, you will be the dots of light
My soul my soul shooting to you

When can I fly this plane
Meeting you in the Milky Way
Two dots of love
Meeting you
Falling into our shooting star

When will I be moonbeams inside the moon
And shine only for you
Two shadows in shadow
Calling from paradise near and far

Going to roll down the hill into death
I will not die
Going to roll down the hill
Going to catch the wildflowers as I go
Going to fall between the stones
What is up may be down
No one knows
But you
Yes, you will be the unvanquished night
My dear unknown
My heaven

We Do Not Know What God Has in Store

We do not know what God has in store
The precious things are cut down
One rung at a time

We are the frame with no picture
Swallowed by gravity
Yet I touch without my eyes
And know you before the first brush
The stroke and blush

I can graze the glass
Sink my fingers into it
As if its surface were made to be entered
The hardness caves into your mercy

Loving you
I remember every world
I have ever lived
I inhabit every body I ever was
As you say in one day, in one night
Years ago and centuries
That you are still your dust
Even the tears of our eyes are not our own

All my tears could write you poetry
Kiss them

The words are yours
From your lips
Made mine

Spirit: The Shared Poems of Artist Carol Scott & Caitlin Smith Gilson

Grand Chandelier, **by Carol Scott**

When the Ghost of Me Comes

When the ghost of me comes
To take my body through the hills
Will I become a rush of white dandelion
Blown by you
Every particle something connected to you
Drifting with no need of purpose
Only the essence of your lifeforce
Breathing on me
All wishes coming true

Kisses flying while I am dying
Burning embers
Starstruck heavens
Waiting for me
Was it yesterday?

I am the phantom
Newly formed
Looking and praying
For where I belong
Meaning
Vanitas
Fingers hopeful to touch love
Welcome home

The ghost of me came
And took my body home
With every awestruck
Opened jaw
Knee clutched
Trembling gasp
Skyward eyes
Circus tent
Trapeze act
Dismount leaping

Sweet apparition of death
Close to God's shadow
This is the irony of ends
The final things
The loving place
Blown out lion's teeth
Waxen white
Floating sunlight
If I could *be* this for you
I would
Riveting spice
Into the line itself
Miracle in dying
Thanksgiving

Today When I Left

Today when I left
My soul anchored itself in the passing image
Dredging the ocean floor

You glide across my surface
Sleek unbroken thick
Impermeable line
Pure reflective silver in waveless water

Life is not long
Soundless song of my soul
It haunts and twists
This field of vision tunneling felt unseen
Edges of you in black jet night
Heightened luminescent core
Your gravitational lure
Flowing from nowhere
Everywhere

I see the universe
Your eyes my eyes
Complex ecosystem
As above so below

The sense of being somewhere near
Such intensity of you

As fragrance passed
Through hair fallen waterfall
Cascaded veil of shoulders stilled

Life is one shuttering touch
Peering through to the other side
Cradlesong lullaby trace of me
You will be and I will know you
Persistent as you are

I see the universe
Your eyes my eyes
Complex ecosystem
As above so below

Your complexion
A breviary of sacred prayer
Codas of need seen and felt
Candle read shadow
Hymns and hours
Psalm spoken lovers laying down
Enclosed in the other
Singing your low tone
The unearthed hum
The vibration of my heart
I did not know
My eyes
I did not know
These tears
I did not know
Life is not long

Crystal ball tell us all
Falling water wash us fresh

Flies of fire play
Make beauty
We grieve the dead
Way of nature
Forced
Tides cannot be turned
Flow with the flow
Persistence fades

I die to the universe
Your eyes my eyes
Complex ecosystem
As above so below

Lines in Water

You are the mystery of the poem
That is the sacredness of you
Through every written word
Charms from your sweetest body

Your face
Waves white caps in ecstasy

My revenant heart overflows
Bleeds out love
All tributaries of my beating body
Into my breathing
Into the weight of my head
The wonder of one human soul
Greater than all the world

You turned the muscle of my heart
Into all feeling
This is a love song
A song of love
All the way down
Through every written word
Every time sight was not enough

Light shifts into new shapes
Songs vibrating

Patterns flapping
Bubbling crashing the edges
Blown across your shoulders

Your face
Waves white caps in ecstasy

You are all line and form
That breaks batters shatters the center
I rub my eyes to take in the glimpse
To catch your silhouette
Passing steeply into me
Music harmonizing in strength
Gentleness listening, feeling
Surrounding colliding
Creating rings that spread
With one drop baptized in love

Your face
Waves white caps in ecstasy

We are thieves in bliss
Arresting time from time
Suspending the verse
Held unmatched
Until the chord descends discreetly
Your forever mystery
This is my love song
A song of love
For you
All of me on your floor
Your tint suspended in a ground

Your face
Waves white caps in ecstasy

IMAGINE UTOPIA: *The Sextet*

I. You Ask and I Say

The soul is the body
The body is the soul
I look at you and it is always you
Your soul is your body

When I weep
That is my body
It is my soul
You only have to ask
And I will always say

When I look at your body
I love the soul of you
Undying perfect shot
Aimed before time
God's hands all over you

You only have to ask
And my soul will receive
I would rip up the floorboards to find you
your body is your soul

II. You Are Constellation

I lay at the base of your back
You crack me open
Unbroken

All the fireflies
Of every world
Here around us

My breasts upon your back
Your affinity soft and firm
Floating into ether

Rising candles in infinite paper lanterns
I know this is to be my soul
I know that it could find you anywhere
You are constellation
The God knowing
The God trusting
The God praying

God's hands all over you
You are constellation

III. All Words Are from My Soul

You have a way of pulling your lips close
Lithe alarm bells perched together
A foreshadowed bliss
You do this when you are amused
When loving yourself
When you have that single perfect phrase

You know your own worth and your lips acquiesce
Your body
Your sexed body is your soul

My being, my flesh
It misses you in ways
That it could command oceans
All the waves depart
The waves part and let me pass
To the earth's confession
When it was first made
But still you are too far away

All words are from my soul
Every feeling is my soul
Experiences

IV. Sensual Ripening of the Fruit of You

Your soul
Fingers to the honey pot
The unbroken knot

Your art is your body
Your art is your soul
Your art is alive

Fertile for years

All earth formed inside your soul
Your body is spent sigh
Water fallen joints
Enjoying

Coming with gravity
Sensual ripening of the fruit of you

Sparkling fire torque
Fallen maple leaves
Caramelized baked apple
Cinnamon butter cooling
Fingers licked
Spellbound steep of your breast to bone

Your art is word
Your art is flesh
Your art is life

Fertile for years
Sensual ripening of the fruit of you

V. Perfection of the Perfect One

You alone have the power
To take the miles of my quick
Ten twenty thirty forty miles of slick
Lingering basking scents and sounds
A violet-colored meteorite
Crashing down
All embodied
All soul

Grace and goodness and fun
Perfection of the perfect one

Your low-strung syllable leapt
The long enunciated want
Unkept kiss

You have this way with your lips
When you are amused
Aroused
You can push those hips
All the way down

I have my teeth on your waist
Hurricane maker
Body breaker

Grace and goodness and fun
Perfection of the perfect one

Singing is for you
Sighing is for you

Loving myself is loving you

Beauty is for you
Rapturous thoughts are for you
Heavenly thoughts are saved for you
Loving thoughts are love
You

You are the being of me

I feel deeply passionately
Our souls have fused

I am in you
From the tip of my head to the soles of my feet
You are in me from the soles of your feet to the tip of your head
Communion
Blessed goodness

One voice

Grace and goodness and fun
Perfection of the perfect one

VI. Into the Well of Your Voice

When I heard you sing that day
Dropped down barrel
Into the well of your voice
You could pinch me and I would melt
Sweltering heat
Yelp and howl
Lapping up the salt of your push

The rise of you so smooth
You could shock water
Your call and response
My slunk-down sugary pull
Into the well of your voice
You could pinch me and I would melt

We speak
A language unknown
A language without translation
I think we do

You finish me
I finish you

I think of my death one day
This is not morbid talk
It is the way of realization
The way of rest
We are so graced
Blessed to know the other
To have the other in our sights
On our kiss
In our touch

When I heard you sing that day
Could you hear me sighing?

The way we laugh the same
You are with me in your laughter
In the before and the after

You work
You move
You consider

Liquid spun silk web
Watching you
Watching me

I work
I move
I consider

We have transported ourselves into the beloved
When we come

Together
Wells of your voice are mine
Your thinking and feeling collide
My thinking and feeling collide

We work in texture
We move in air
We consider the other in ourselves

When you heard me sing that day
I could hear you sighing

What Makes Me Hold On

What makes me hold on
To the night eyes
Open
Avoiding sleep
Every thought
Draped along the winding sheet
The inquiries of my mind
The things done and undone

Daydreaming
When I should be night dreaming

Rock my soul in slumber
Angelic blessing of love tonight
Painter of epiphany
Dream adventuresome dream
Rolling smile divinity
Blindfolded doubt
Tomorrow is sooner than now

You are the arc of creation
The strength of foundation
The world untold
Love directs your sensation
Your movement is consecration

This is what makes you hold on
To the night eyes
Open
You are the now
The lost hope found
The future grace
The eternal play
Tomorrow in the foothold of today

Not to Be Left Behind

Not to be left behind
I quickened my step
Not to make you sad
I agreed

Questions led me
Answers beckoned me
Indecision became decision
Fear turns actions to ice
Frozen
Life births a hero
When the stakes are more important
Than the self

If I stay
Rhythm
Dancing unison
Rainbows turn to sun
Playing made better

If I stay too long
I burn
Even in night
Struggling
Praying always

Where is the line and the limit?
The staying and the going?
Between the near and the far
I do not know

I am twirling a loop of infinity
Destined to repetition striving
End over end
Over

We are offerings to the gods
Leave yourself
There is laughter and smiling
This is the other side

You Have All the Power

You have all the power
I am love in your arms
Folded ornamental planes of bright color

Will you feed me, sting me
Make me the fruit of the tree
Return me, unearth me
Let me race the setting sun

Descending shafts touch your face
You tapered in all lambent north
Bless me, rest me
Light absorbing light
Fog becoming fog
In the chasm of my mind
Wondering I cannot see

You have all the power
Growing bigger, luminous stars
Senses of you in the dark
Want for you in unclothed honesty
Your sex without inhibition
Challenging gamesmanship
Running and tackling across the sky
I hear the thunderous roar of your laughter
Be my pleasure

Holy Saturday

You cannot imagine what sorrow and anger seize one's whole soul when a great idea, which one has long and piously revered, is picked up by some bunglers and dragged into the street, to more fools like themselves, and one suddenly meets it in the flea market, unrecognizable, dirty, askew, absurdly presented, without proportion, without harmony, a toy for stupid children.

—Dostoevsky, *Demons*

Between Heaven and Earth, by Carol Scott

Of Ancient Oracles: From Good Friday to the Harrowing

My soul is stoned in silence
I know and it is done
So terribly unhappy and more terribly alone

Not long ago
You were thrust on your sword and your larkspurs grew
Prussian blue delphinium, and each an unbranched stalk . . .

Not long ago
I was knit together in my mother's womb, unhidden from you
Made in the secret place
You know full well the depths of the mantle
Vandal of metamorphoses and sorrow
These leaves are three-toothed lobes in palmate shape
And you
Once oceanic and free
Divinity of risen and fallen sea
All salt robed in green beyond Thebes
When the son is the father, and the father is the son
There were such things
Now these roots go lower than the flower
Descending sleep and never wake
This body has no counterweight

Save me, O God, the waters have come in, even unto my soul

Pinned white bird coo for me
With feather tips trimmed in silver
Caladrius of little death and ecstasies
The caves have their own arteries
Carved long before I was born

Threefold dove on shorn winter's cliff
Will you look into my face pinned as you are
I cannot see, filled with shame
I never knew how to be
Where are the roots of the flowering tree?
If only your gaze would come again
So that I may live and die and live without sin

Not long ago
You were thrust on your sword and your larkspurs grew
Prussian blue delphinium, and each an unbranched stalk . . .

Your Cross is staked earth
Marsyas in agony
Shoulder wrought in ivory
You are the lost child encased in burnt clay
How will you ever see the day
Numberless Eurydices skinned by the sun
Deadheaded bud below the earth
Chthonic offering of you and you
Confusion of myth and dream and you
How can you save me, pallid delphinium
Inflorescence among the weed
Acheron's waters you feed

Save me, O God, I have drifted into deep waters, where the flood engulfs me

This embankment must erode
The twofold door below
Cardea's hinges rattling but I cannot get through
There is no verb, the word is soundless fear
Marching on hollowed marrow
Too near too near too near to run

Splintered knee turned inside out
Cup of my bone and stoned silence
Wormwood tear
I know and it is done
Too near to near too near to run

Plummeting from cypress
Woven from knitted rope
So terribly unhappy and more alone
Red ruined delphinium
Too near to near too near to run

Not long ago
My children, their eyes hollowed out forest
If only I could cover them
Galateas in flesh
If only they could be covered
Myrmidons free from sickness unto death
But I am dying in my own recollection
Diminishing star still sighted but gone
And it is beyond wishes these needful things
Ants drown in the sugar of the blood
Too little too little too little loved
Save me, Oh God, I am weary from my crying and my throat is parched

If only we could swim
Where is the raft, God, the one you promised

If only the waters were frozen
If only it was a teardrop this torrent
But my soul is washed in silence

Why did you form me without food
Without light, in the matter of a star
Nurse of the end
Where is the air
Airless dome of my voice

If only I could breathe
Where is the air, God, you promised when you gave me life
No crown of angels
Where is the land?
Where is the dove descending
Where is the earth you promised
And the happy ending

Bodies in quicksand
And my children cannot swim
Cannot sink, cannot breathe
What is to be done?
No treading Leanders, no straits to pass

Where is the earth you promised
And the air?
Where are the seas with salt that feed our tears?
Formed and formed and formed without bread, without air!
Formed without the leavened stare
When you take the sword
To my throat and cut my hair
Then perhaps then
I can breathe your air

If only your hands were here
If only I knew my eyes in sleep
Unbroken legs hanging from the tree
The last life cut for your final deed
And the vine at my lips tightly knit
Vandal of metamorphoses and sorrow
These leaves are three-toothed lobes in palmate shape
Saturday will not lift this violet cape

Not long ago
You were thrust on your sword and your larkspurs grew
Prussian blue delphinium, and each an unbranched stalk . . .

How can we be made to love as fragile as we are
Damastes died that night
His body made to fit the iron bed
Stretching and cutting the legs
Wounds at every side
His body made and crushed and never made again
Pinned white bird sing for me
Pinned as you are

Oh My God, save me, insults have broken my heart, and I am in despair

Not long ago
You kissed me without touching my skin
I cannot live without your kiss
I place my lips to the candle and it burned
Supplicant of my loss

Not long ago
You died rolled in stone
And the wires that were my vessels
Transporting my inner shipwreck

Became a knotted anchor
Furies at the bottom of the sea

If you would breathe on me again, then I would breathe
If you could touch me again, then I could touch
But if you bury me, how can I love as fragile as I am
Larkspur nourished on the blood of the lamb

And all the mean and wicked tales will those go with you to the tomb?
Themis and Theia in doom and death, into the sorrow of your keeping
And all the sorcery and the magic, the quick death, and the nourishment
The fall of the Titans, Elysium, and all apology
Will they be with you deep in the cacophony
Oracle of the end
Adamantine sickle hanging from the tree
If you bury me, how can I love you as fragile as I am

Not long ago
You were thrust on your sword and your larkspurs grew
Prussian blue delphinium, and each an unbranched stalk . . .

Growling winged tiger
Jawing the lunar creature
Apollo atrophied in whiplash
What wisdom can there be
I am living on your breathing, and I cannot go on

Why can't I hold you cold as I am
Your face is made of fire and flower
Your body a temple, an altar sheathed in gold
I am living on your breathing, and I cannot go on

Here is the darkest house of Hades
Deucalion below the surface

No waves, no movement
Here the last particles of the earth collide
This is the torn cloth
The split temple of our being
Every confusion contused into one
I know it is done
I am living on your breathing, and I cannot go on

I know the sadness I cannot know
Lover cloak and wrap me
Open and close me
If only I could taste the chosen fragrance
To be winding cloth
Broken hollow bones thin as darning needles
Tightly knit
And the oil of my tears your inebriation

Oh My God, save me, I looked for sympathy, but there was none

Not long ago
My hundred dips and dives washed your sides
My hundred dips your innocence
Hundreds of eyes
Argus in peacock's tail
A hundred eyes to watch over you
And I have formed you, knitted you, with my colliding star
My hundred indentations, this lip-taken water and wine
Your eyes sky-blue delphinium and you wash my sides
There is no snow beneath me, never will I melt

If only your gaze
If only you will look into my face a hundred times
A hundred cycles of the earth
My face, your face, a hundred upon a hundred days

This homing bird fed on winter berry
Come home
This is the time of need
The time of a hundred eyes
My time cannot comfort
Scentless deadheaded delphinium

Lovers make love unable to break free from time
It chains them and I am chained
Made from clay and chained to the ends of the earth
To the ends of the earth, we are the winding sheet
The steep embankment
The spun honey
Raise the bowl, food of the gods
Ants stuck in the sugar of the blood

Come with me where there is air and earth
Come with me to far away land
But what, my love, my Passiontide
Could change the course of the moon and tide
Greyest fields of Asphodel
We are damned and knitted tight
We are bruised in the first kick in the womb
Cut in grief
Greed of my peace
Stone of the tomb
This body
      Your body
           Your nectar
                Has no counterweight

Oh My God, save me, I looked for comforters, but I found no one

I Did Not Know

There has always been pain
Square lodged in circle
Downed in strangulated spiral stair
The edges force the soft curve
Puncturing the inner drum
Till the *once was* cannot go on

Pain is the song and the virtue
The everlasting liar
The collapsed freighted craving
The scorched desire

The working body is this scraped out hour
Weakened vessels
Masses of failure this heart
Curled in on itself
Bounding towards the indefinite tense

Pain is the soul's election slid into body
The extremity and all its causation
The whiplash and the consecration
Every untethered end

This is the set and the match
The founding soil before the seed
Loss casts what it will

Shipwrecked fatigued dream
Sucked bitter charcoal
Sunk in underwater sand
Untouched by sun
Till the *once was* cannot go on

Pain is frayed rope
The lost divinity
The metal on the tongue
The rupture, never young

I did not know the order
The sequence
The rule
I did not know the nectar
The straw of the flower
The way from garden to garden
The lands and fields
All dotted stone pathways
Homes with doors and window light
I did not know

The Night of Fresh Squeezed Lemons

Do not worry about me
We are beyond sorrow here
Only the unknown variable remains
And we can see that through
Together

You know by now
The shot ribbons streamed relief
The madness of angels
The spreading center
I come in fractions
Elections of longing

You keep me
Sweeping the peach
Lingering showered steam
Attended condensation
Stabbing muscled pang
The final transfer of energy
The difference and the same

I can sweat the sunset
It has no power over us
Sliced open yellows crushed
If only your scent stayed longer on my hair

You put your body in place of my fear
Light pours, pours from your kiss
What will become of us
If we keep loving as we do?

It Was Only One Sunset Ago

It was only one sunset ago
That your body fell into mine
As draped garment
All given silk

Even in tonight's loneliest rose
I can smell the cherry blossoms
That came between us
When sun climbed your skin

The light re-drew the boundaries of your body
Floating substance descending and rising

Tonight
I am shivering in my skin
Too cold to move
Wreckage of time and hope
Tonight
If I fall asleep too soon
Will you wake
Tonight
If I drift from the steeple
Will I walk into night
And drop into the sea

If only your memory was your body
If only your soul was also mine
If only the sun would never dip low
If only there was nothing below the earth
If only it was one sunset ago

The Spirit

I will be there
To entrance the ease and glide
To trail my fingers into the shallow depressions
That make your skin the blushed coral effigy
Feed your scent as necklace
Hint of collarbone

Of Hell

I am all sin
Fool's deliverance
No eternal spring
Rotting inside, wings made of stone
When I crumble
And I will
It will be alone

The Dead Sea

The dipped center of Testament and Sea
This is my heart
Ready to be sifted
To be revived with your tear
Cooler than air

I am a scattered artifact
Before silvered pans
Sift the sand
I am the eternal return returning to you

Wherever there is sunset or sunrise
Light coming and waning
I am and you are
The descending fingers of my center
I your undertow
You my soul

We are steeped in your power
Held in surrender
Rebuilt in the other
I cherish the wilds of you
The untamed toll of night
The anger and the peace
The verve of your force

Your spirit exhales and gives me
The spinning merry-go-round
All light faster than sound

You are the sheath of the knife
The perilous life
The pure cut
The cure
You excise the dead
And bring me to life

Raised rotating platform of you
Always you
And I am I
Nothing but love and offering

I know you
I know you and it is all love

There Is Only Love and Time

There is only love and time
If we put them too close
It is the pain of angles and ends

Let them stand apart
Day be day
And night be night
Let teardrops be snowfall
Memory be the leaping

One day ago
The horizon came
But I paid it no heed
It will never hurt us
No lengths of unmet need
No measure drifting between
Our seasons are made of overripe fruit
The rivers never flood

There is only love and time
If we put them too close
Edges
Contours
Raining again

Disjecta Membra

The passing sense of losing you
If it stayed would crush me

I would be the grit of bodies burned
With all their trappings
Burned out hidden exit
The pressure would be instantaneous
Collapsed high rise imploding in on itself
Or as wounded animal
Disjecta membra
Crouched in corner awaiting its own end

The passing sense of losing you
If it stayed would crush me

All spirit and memory limping on the roadside
The sense of losing you
You beyond my sight
Beyond memory and hope
Bands of black steel
This sting of losing you
Longing affliction unable to compete
This sense unearthed
This gasping gaze
If it remained

I would become
Carbonized petrified stone

The passing sense of losing you
If it stayed would crush me

Lover are you passing through?
Before the passing station
Passed on by
I did not understand
How these things slip away

Lover are you passing through?
I thought I could hold on
All dissipated sensation
Smuggling even
The memory of touch

Lover are you passing through?
Before and before
I gave myself over
Sheltered in you
But it has passed and I
I am nowhere to be found

The passing sense of losing you
If it stayed would crush me

You Have Taken My Child

You have taken my child and I wept
Were they not enough?
Those tears fed the blackthorns each spring
They flourished just as you asked
A brutal sacrifice
Angelus lighter than air

I dreamt my children's faces in profile
The morning after the fall
Quiescent rings of icing and blue frosted boat
A shoreline of shorn shells cutting our soles
The bells of Gudalupe miles beyond sight
Our lives dying in us bleeding underfoot
River of the wolf
Floating side by side under untouched sun

I should have grown old when you thieved my child
The weight of you in last temptation
You snatched my hands, my lips, my time
Lungs sponged with the matter of your blood

I should have gone cold when you stole my child
Thief in the night
Broken idea, denier of earth and sky
Confused shards plunged in wine

Remove this taste of the gall
God of night
God of the inner law
My lips withdraw
But you keep stealing the gentler things of my seeking
How can I love if you thieve all my sweetness?

I am your emptied verse and vessel
A rehearsal without a play
Lion without a lamb
Lines without verb
Grains of shoal
Wasteland of your long-call echo

You have taken my child
The blanket flower, buttercup, and lupine
The common poppy and baby blue eye
You cannot find my soul
The home of my sleep is made of coal
But long ago it was once my own
And still you stand beside the bed ready to roll away my love, my stone of heaven

The Pinched Outer Shell

Lover I never seek to hurt you
I may pinch the outer shell
To see that you bleed for me
As I the blood of you
Moons ago when life did not know

Lover I am the gripped groaning of two
Torrents of longing
In the fear of losing you
Moons have past and I
The arriving parting of our time and space
Trials unreplaced the reddened teardrop
An offering, a sacrifice stitched into you
And then back to our grace

I never seek to hurt you love
Only a breeze deep into the matter
For things are sadder than we say
All the ladders rusted away
That day I found you finding me
I have no other place to be but you

You made arms and heart the long reeds to cover me
Your love is the one clarifying good
The escape from the terrible brood
It takes the place of hope

Nothing but God could descend
And I

I am frightened lover
And I know not what to do
The shelter of my soul left one year ago

Below the Altars

You are competing my love against stretches of ice
The brick and mortar of time and space
One moment inside and I perish
A needle in spinning thread

You are competing my love against the brutal ends
The quick fire of the flame
I am intricate battered engine missing the keys

You are competing my love against the rotating axis
With speed it does not cease
But then is your touch
The ways of your compact hold
Radiant mind made into peace
Anywhere and nowhere in you

You are competing my love against the world and its terrible lies
All lowered language below the altars
But your touch rains down comets
You stall the setting sun

Be the turning, the combustion and sparks
I am the dying down dying
Given to you

God, I want lay between your sheets tonight
There is no race no competition
There is only you
Your touch stalling the sunset

The sheets could be made of sackcloth, woven straw, and un-spun wool
But they would rest me in your mercy
Dragonfly over stilled thread

What then could I give you?

Holy Saturday: The Shared Poems of Artist Carol Scott & Caitlin Smith Gilson

The Angel of Sorrow, by Carol Scott

Seven Last Words

You greet the first sun without guise
All known forsaken and ready to die
One arctic sanderling before the fowler's snare
And I the fragrance of time's embrace

Trapped guided to the end divine despair
A hallowed Samson cut in his sleep
Tree-holding God in deep final breath
And I the fortune of Eden's embrace

Hearing your call, feeling locked your face
Powerless to part the seas, your lips
Love and hate me with sinning lies
And I the future of time's embrace

Folded form, your beauty the nail's edge
Shrouded in darkness surrendering the promised life
My ribs became these knees for you
And I the force of Eden's embrace

All you all world perfected by faith
Every ring of the tree the sap
History written in wood crucified to resurrection
And I the flowering of time's embrace

My face is flesh warmed by flame

Your seven words sweeten the sinking Son
Blood of blood, tomb of Holy Saturday
And I the fate of Eden's embrace

This Unexpressed Heart

This unexpressed heart
Lives only to slow its beat
Miles deep into the said
Seven on seven miles
Down into the trench

This unexpressed heart
Lives only to slow its beat
I love you
Every collapsed card of me

If time is slowed will our time increase?
If time is speed will our time be lost?

Remake the physical divide
Erode as roads disappear in volcanos
As seas over time claim the rocks that dot
The shoreline past my windows
Breeze of the bed

Give me time my love
Give me time
Break the bread
Give me time

Racing time and time is slowing
Heart hugged to the backbone
Together and apart
Spinning human sextile
A flat circle hooped orbiting the other

You are the counting
The measure
You occupy this carbon black silo
You are Ganymede in exile
The silent storehouse
The beating muscle dying down
You command my soul
The riches of my being
The poverty of every dream

If time is slowed will our time increase?
If time is speed will our time be lost?

When the Colors Come

When the colors come and the form appears
Art blooms
Freedom runs the sacred
Paradisal somersaulting orange and gold
The sun has nothing on this yellow
In the Saturday of waiting

Lay down your soul
The weighting anchor
The burden
The crush
Only the colors
The lovers
The light of the Cross

Fireplace of the heart
Life and heat
Bold vision of pink
Drummers beat
Melody undefined
Crucified under the same sky

Hypnotic repeat
Enrapturing the spirit
Unchained in the flow
Someday

Some days push till bad becomes good
In the tomb of waiting

When the form appears
Communion with the divine
The color of music for eye and soul
See and hear my song
Touch my sides

This is life
All the turns
The beauty and the loss
The good of living
The soul can bear
The body too
Love is infinite salve
The paradise of you

Life Is Surface

Life is surface
Protective skin deep
Largest organ of the body

Underneath structure of strength
Muscle of mastery
The being of you
Anger
Calm
Place of thoughts

Anywhere you touch the surface is felt
Hairs raise and react

Life is skin
Squeezed
Held
Played
The skin of lips
The nearness of bones risen to the surface
The soft convex of the belly
The scent when skin invades skin
The window of you

Site of remorse
Point of genius

Chair of emotion
Mover to the doer

How do I know?
Question upon questions
Experienced through flesh

What I Mean to Say

What I mean to say
Is that happiness with you
Is at a point that goes beyond itself
Into an aching joy it has no power to enter
Knowing and doing
Wanting and having

It is the kind of happiness
That's become self-aware
It knows itself as experience
Our happiness is looking at itself
Passing the windowed mirrors
Yielding to the one true one
Smiling need
To be part of you
Braided to your muscle
Transfused to your blood

What I mean to say
Is that this happiness
Brings me to the point of tears
But to none ever shed
Life seasoned with salt

I cannot read the form
Only the thought of the tear

Stays right there
To the left and right of my heart
It pulls closer
Behind my orbit
The pressing of this happiness
It exceeds the boundary line
So far beyond what I have felt
It can only make itself

You bring me to the point of no return
I am found with you
Something stained
More than lost
If this happiness could not remain

You bring me between
Heaven and Eden
Ever-running song
Waterfalls and wild dives
Into cascades of ice
And breathing is all the more real
Your air is the inhalation of my lungs
Bringing life being us

The world of your love
Spirit made earth
As blades of grass as rain
As plucked fruit
As your lips
Food for my salvation

You are bringing me to a place
In the spirit life
I can leave my body at night

And come to you
My soul which has no matter
Somehow touches your nakedness
And we sink
You the waking
The laughter
The feeling of being
Becoming life again

Never send me back to my body
You can make my body out of yours
And we will be forever
The lovers

POSTSCRIPT

Easter Sunday

Her heart felt as if it were breaking in her breast, bleeding and bleeding, young and fierce. From grief over the warm and ardent love which she had lost and still secretly mourned; from anguished joy over the pale, luminous love which drew her to the farthest boundaries of life on this Earth. Through the great darkness that would come, she saw the gleam of another, gentler sun, and she sensed the fragrance of the herbs in the garden at world's end.

—Sigrid Undset, *Kristin Lavransdatter II: The Wife*

The Invitation of the King—Rex 1890, by Carol Scott

In the Time and Sky of You

In the time and sky that is forever you
I was young and I looked to the vista
To the setting sun of king's amethyst and irradiating citrine
Before the black of quartz-bonded stars cradled my head
As crown of evening dreaming rambling streets
Did I remember then what it is to fall on the sword of your touch
And become all blood and water

You know what it is to look far and wide to the water and sky
Into the thicket of azured gravity
But I did not see you then
I knew the twinkling gilded diamonds of other homes in other towns
Across the bay where you were hidden away
Farther than the sting of the sword of your touch
All giving and easing
Back then I was the twinkling of limestone given by the moon

Did you hear my steps as I walked within your long-timed breathing
We are respirating strings corseted by whale bones
Across centuries of steam and sighs
You are bound to me these ropes and sinews
Whitecaps lashed hand and foot of our Odyssey

My love is the lamb shaved for its wool
The marble balcony soaring above this painted land
The lonely sonata of seafaring ships

The garden gate and the house within
My love is time and sky

When I fell on the sword of your touch
I became all blood and water
All giving and easing
To gain the forever yours
I do this in memory of you

Baptismal Font

All I am
Is the penetrating basin
Pressed amber clay
Layered mantle of ancient perishing
Filled with love for you

And I am
The bone collector's pain
The drowned stone
Rubbed into circulation
Smoother than heated incline plane

And I am
The inviolate figure shock of the wound
The stealth of your hour
The interest of watchmen
Damascus in ivory

Don't you know
This rain bathes us on loan
Dissolves even the stone
You cannot survive
Supple as you are

Ground me down in mortar and pestle
Crush me into powder

Paste made with your tears
Lick of your lips on mine
The heart's pull hides in marbled veins
I am
Unseen geometry
Unfelt angle
Undone ringer of bells
Set among the sugar cubes

Do not go
Into the storehouse
Do not go
There is no air
No sails no sun
Break my bread
Drink my wine
Stake the flesh of me
Thin white body round
Deed of the deadhead
Mater Dei rose red
Blood and watershed
Cast on the eve of time

And you
Do this in memory of me

Easter Vigil

Tonight, I will imagine you sleeping
Cradled into yourself
In the silence of night

Your voice is the clearing
All hoping and being
Reverberating hollowed metal
You can do anything to me

I will love you and love you and love you

I can be asleep and awake with ease
Your image is all imprint of heat and silver
Warmer shades of red wax
Pressed into my keeping

I can transport myself into dream
Your sacred hovering above mine
The space between us becoming ether

I will love you and love you and love you

I know you will soon descend
Rendering me bound
Embraced in tidal wave
You can do anything to me

You Need a Love Song

You need a love song
Words spun from the web of my soul
Retrieving the very good
The Beauty of you

Here are the taken strings
Between the world material and spirit
And made touch
They shine in your light water hush

I follow the strings all the way
To the center of me
And I bring it to the center of you
Pure song

This is my love song
The word
The good
The crossed windowpane
Every drawn curtain
The pulled back bed
The spun sheet
The drink doused in ice
Hot drawn baths
This ineluctable look
This clutched embrace

I sink into wilderness
It is all and forever you

When I move my legs
It is you gliding across me
When I breathe
It is your rhythm within mine

I think you are grace itself
I think you could save me
You devouring me

You are the taste of time
You are earthless, shadowless glass
Centuries of music
Hidden to all but my mind and yours

To love you beyond the signifiers
The forever, the ever, and the after
You can take the modifiers with your eyes
Your hands are my clothes
The shelter of your skin
I am what I am and I am yours
The song of you

My heart is a font made in waterless lands
I would drown
Drown in fire
Freeze in the desert
Starve in paradise without you

Under my breath
I hum the tune of you
Your sound bracing my thighs

You are every electric sky
Every crashing satellite

Even in spirit
You are more than ghost
You make memory present
Tongue on the Host

This is the love song for you
I will play it again
I will never forget
I will always sing
This love for you is all of me

Beyond the Orchids

To say it as it is
I am relieved you are here
Into my soul
You are here
Teardrops are prisoners of sorrow
Mine are something else
All carnal yet unearthly unmerited joy
All the embedded parts of me
Even where my fingers bend are relieved

I have taken and given
Removed and filled
Extinguished and lighted
I am at peace conquered by you
That is love
To be willing captive
Captivated
Freed and remaining

When I unlock you
Your inner lower back bridges our muscles
The electrified spools of skin
All these touches
Are the cherishing
You go beyond the orchids

Easter Sunday: The Shared Poems of Artist Carol Scott & Caitlin Smith Gilson

Splendid, by Carol Scott

You Will Always Be the Delectation

You will always be
The dancing, curving, diving, tonguing delectation of my need
The ice relief on battered knee
The stinging sweet honeybee folded downstream
One endless hush and buzz
Eternity

You will always be
The candy out of the box
No more flavor of the day
Soup du jour, blue plate special
You are exceptional
Perpetual adoration and peace
Four leaves on every clover
The fragrance arranged
Eternity

You will always be
Flowers mingled in the air
Silkworm hair
Brave uncontrolled and free
Laughter
Eternity

Your will always be
Spontaneous Self

Mooning reflections
Shadows casting
Partial Revelations
Brush and touch
Cool hot naked and new
Eternity

I Have Asked You to Haunt Me

I have asked you to haunt me . . .

I have asked you
To haunt me
The rest of my life
Until my lips are blue
Your blue

Ghost of the lines of my palm
Come to me
I am in faraway lands
Endless dawn

Haunt my soul
The rest of my life
Until my eyes become
Reflected sun

Be beside me as I tire
Burnt out wildfire
Farther into the covers I sink
Darkest iron of Eden's gate
Haunt me
In my garden of green
Unseen thief of dream

Haunted my body
Until my calves stretch
Reaching you
Between the blue
The yellow
The sea
Drink me in every mellowed wine
There ever was and will be
Till day is done

When I die do not be sad
Feel me in the breeze of the wind
The smell of jasmine
The taste of a fine martini
In roaring laughter
In the scream of fear

How could I leave you
In life our souls touched in the love of chosen friendship

I will haunt you
Awake or asleep
I will haunt your soul
I will haunt your dreams
In the words you write

When our days are done
I will be so bold
As to ask you to join me in heaven
Two saints having fun

Time and Birth

Do I miss you so because of the day
Or was my day rough because I missed you so?

Moonlight bright to see your smile
Of all reflections I remember yours
Of all touches I feel yours
Of all wants I want you

In my silence your voice echoes
In your words worlds awake
Yell or whisper

In us together life is new
It figures that in living
Happy and sad
Make a home
The same home

Do we age because of sin?
Is time passing because we can no longer endure time?
I must remember you as you are
Will you remember me as I should be
When love toppled towers and made kingdoms into sand?

Sometimes I think we are walking into quicksand
Other times there is fruit on the vine

And I hold on
Words of you saving me

As I grow old I am younger
I am newer in the newness of life
Exuberant of breath
Living a freshness that comes with age
Progressed with a novelty of having been
With still my being questionable
A dreaminess of outer reach
Without pretense or guile
Smiling for the adventure to come
Persistent in this earth
Bang, battered, and bruised
Laughing
Feeling the love
Coming came better
Still I hear
Here I am
Songs are sung
This is the day it began
The day I was born anew

Lagniappe

So much has been said, O Queen of the Apostles, we have lost the taste for discourse, we have no more altars but yours, we know nothing but a simple prayer. All that everywhere else demands an examination, here is but the effect of a defenceless youthfulness. All that everywhere else requires postponement, here is but a present fragility. All that everywhere else demands certification, here is but the fruit of a poor tenderness. All that everywhere else requires a touch of skill, here is but the fruit of a humble ineptitude. All that everywhere else is imbalance, here is but measure and grading. All that everywhere else is a hut, here is but a solid and lasting dwelling-place. All that everywhere else is constriction by the rule, here is but an impetus and abandonment. All that everywhere else is a harsh penalty, here is but a weakness that is relieved. All that everywhere else would be a great effort, here is but simplicity and quiet. All that everywhere else is the wrinkled rind, here is but the lymph and the tears of the vine.

All that everywhere else is a twisting, here is but a release and defencelessness. All that everywhere else is a contraction, here is but calm and silent involvement. All that everywhere else is a degradable good, here is but quiet and rapid disengagement. All that everywhere else is a rigidity, here is but a rose and a footprint in the sand. All that everywhere else is questioned and taken up, here is but a clear river near the source. O Queen, it is here that every soul comes

Like a young warrior fallen by the wayside. All that everywhere else is a steep road, O Queen reigning in your royal court, star of the morning, Queen of the last day, all that everywhere else is the table laid, all that everywhere else is the sense of the road travelled, here is but a serene and firm detachment, and in a temple of calm, far from the flat anxiety, the expectation of a death more alive than life.

—Charles Péguy, *La Tapisserie de Notre-Dame*

Cock's Crow, by Carol Scott

Always Being Told My Eyes Are Beautiful

By Carol Scott

Always being told my eyes are beautiful
If they are the windows of the soul
It must follow
My widows are clean
Perception precise
Vision device

But . . .

What do I see?
What holds in my mind of memory?
Biting eyes
Observing too much
Rather not have seen
Sight that cries out in tears

Unobtrusive yet glimpsed
Not worth looking

If you would see what these eyes have seen
Would you see what I saw?

Longing for reflection
Light
Delight

Most brilliantly bright
Twinkling orbs of wondrous sights
Smiling eyes
Draw me into yours
Where we will share our dreams
Dawning the site of souls

For My Mother

By Caitlin Smith Gilson

Time cannot go on
Being the measure of sunken ships
Unsettled seabeds fending off gravity

The last time that I was
Time was angular and instrumental
Time thrusts itself into its chest
And feeds its young
What are you now that you cannot be?

This is the sadness of inland seas
Of worn bodies of water
Bordered by marsh

I am having trouble with time
Of understanding heaven
Too long a closed circuit
A chamber without echo
A space without distance
A disarmament without a whisper
No raised edge to shave the thorn
What inkling of the sinking stone
Comes to settle close to me

This is the sadness of inland seas
Of worn bodies of water
Bordered by marsh

There is no ghost
No presence in the next room
No legacy
No unremarked verb
I wonder when last I knew
Your measured leagues from home
Silent eyeing storm reading the water
Too lonely for word

This is the sadness of inland seas
Of worn bodies of water
Bordered by marsh

I will never be young and I will never be old
Time propels itself into time
My heart seeps into the wishing well
What are you now that you cannot be?

This is the sadness of inland seas
Of worn bodies of water
Bordered by marsh

Galatea's Kiss

By Caitlin Smith Gilson

Your texture first given is tender
But there is no shelter
You are unpinned elegance
Painted eggshell
Veins of rose gold
Swells of Persian red
A hummingbird tonguing the waterfall
Contours of your geography
But there is no shelter

Every Day Since You Were Born: For Mary & Lily

By Caitlin Smith Gilson

Every day since you were born has been spring
No matter the sorrow

The loss and keeping
The stretched force of fates
My arms open and closing
Down into your home and mine

It is always forever spring my words
Their speaking is spring
Upon your look and touch
The light will never end
Green covers the ground in spring

I am the old of endless tumbling
Of earth giving over its song
It may be winter but I am never lost

You are the long long days of spring
The sun will never fail us
Your warmth that day
The day you were born
Held itself to me
And I was the unknowing one

You were the first time I was
In the time of my spring
The time that I became yours

See the hollow ahead
A road with wild trees
All lush canopies and hedges
In spring, there are bushes of honeysuckle
Their scent is the promise of an oil sweet
It tells you that I am near
It will always be that way
My kisses cover you as honeysuckle
When you sleep and sleep and wake and sleep

My heart is everything that spring is
Do you sight the blossoms bright
Popping pinks
Your cheekbones
Your soft face unmarred by salt and age
Your roundness was that color
The day you were made in my arms
Which is every day when I am
Everything that spring is

Remember I am always with you
Forever thinking
Placing my soul in the shade
In the sun heading your way
Reflecting the days the earth will never end
It will never end and I love you

I love you with everything that is the best in me
And I borrow more from the gods
More love and more spring and more sun

Just to raid your heart with your fragrance
That you give me that day long ago

The God who made you kneaded you into me
Before I was even born
Honeysuckle scent and long rays of sunshine
That first day of May

Full of Grace, by Carol Scott

The Authors

www.ingramcontent.com/pod-product-compliance
Lightning Source LLC
Chambersburg PA
CBHW051107230426
43667CB00014B/2481